P9-DFB-390

Scholastic Guides

Checking Your Grammar

Scholastic Guides

Checking Your Grammar

··

Marvin Terban

SCHOLASTIC
REFERENCE

Illustrations by Peter Spacek

No part of this publication may be reproduced in whole or in part, or stored in a retrieval system, or transmitted in any form or by any means, electronic, mechanical, photocopying, recording, or otherwise, without written permission of the publisher. For information regarding permission, write to Scholastic Inc., Attention: Permissions Department, 557 Broadway, New York, NY 10012.

ISBN 0-590-49455-4

Copyright © 1993 by Scholastic Inc.
All rights reserved. Published by Scholastic Inc.
SCHOLASTIC, SCHOLASTIC REFERENCE, and associated logos are trademarks and/or registered trademarks of Scholastic Inc.

10 9 8 7 6 5 4 3   02 03 04 05 06

Printed in the U.S.A. 09
This edition first printing, August 2002

Contents

Adjectives

Adverbs

Prepositions

Conjunctions

Interjections

Section Three: Style and Usage

Index

Introduction

Has a teacher, parent, or even a friend ever told you that you made a mistake in grammar? Did you wonder how you were supposed to know what was wrong or how to fix it? English is a very beautiful and expressive language. It is also very tricky and loaded with rules and exceptions. This book includes the important grammar rules you need to know and most of those exasperating exceptions.

How can you organize a sentence so it will get across exactly the meaning you want? First, you have to know the parts of a sentence (subject, predicate, clause, phrase, etc.) and the parts of speech (nouns, verbs, adjectives, etc.). If you know the way a word is used, you are more likely to understand what it means. Then, if you use it correctly when you speak or write, people are more likely to know what you mean.

The more you use this, or any other reference book, the more skillful you'll become at finding things quickly. In this book, you can look things up in more than one way. If you know the topic (Pronouns, for instance) you can find where it begins in the Table of Contents on page 5. If you're searching for something more specific (Uses of Personal Pronouns, for example) you can look it up in the Section Table of Contents on page 25. And if you're looking for something more specific (choosing the correct personal pronoun, for example), you can look it up in alphabetical order under Pronouns in the Index at the back of the book. All through the book, you'll see the words *See Also* followed by a page number. They tell you where else in the book there is more information about the same topic.

I've been an English teacher for thirty years, so I know that many students don't like grammar. But I also know that playing with words can be fun. Once you know the rules, you'll be a better writer, reader, speaker, and listener. And—best of all—people will stop saying you're making mistakes once you get into the habit of *Checking Your Grammar.*

Marvin Terban

Twenty Common Grammatical Errors
And How to Fix Them

I don't want no help with this project.
See Preventing Double Negatives, 111

The forgetfull scientist siezed the turkies.
See Good Spelling Rules to Use Every Day, 102

John and me got lost in the mall.
See How to Choose the Correct Pronoun: Subject or Object?, 45

I don't think its going to rain.
See Contractions: Shrinking Words, 127

Sybil's cousin found Dougs umbrellas in the Goldin's car.
See Punctuation Rules Everybody Needs: Apostrophes in Possessive Nouns, 84

At the zoo we saw deers, sheeps, mooses, gooses, and wolfs.
See Forty-One Irregular Plurals, 30

While the hot sun shined, he lied down under a shady tree.
See Ninety Irregular Verbs, 57

The porcupines sneezes.
See Making Subjects and Verbs Work Together: Subject-Verb Agreement, 20

"Can you help me study fractions asked Juan", so I won't fail the math test."?
See Punctuation Rules Everybody Needs: Quotation Marks, 93

In the west they study Science and french all Summer long.
See When and Why to CAPITALIZE a Word, 98

Slipping down the muddy bank and plopping into the river.
See When a Group of Words is not a Sentence: Fragments, 18

This kitten gets even more cuter every day.
See Comparison of Adjectives, 66

Cab driver, please drive more slower and talk loudlier.
See Comparison of Adverbs, 73

There to hungry too weight for they're desert.
See Homonyms: Words That Sound Alike but are Spelled Differently, 115

Be an angle and do what your conscious tells you.
See 100 Easily Confused and Misused Words, 120

The boring movie knocked the audience's socks off.
See Idioms: When Words Mean More Than They Say, 131

Each student should leave his desk.
See Avoiding Sexist Language, 113

The teen ager fastened her seat-belt.
See Building Compound Words, 129

Harriet thought she'd failed, however she got the highest grade.
See Semicolons (Punctuation), 95

At 9:04 A.M., I told the F.B.I. to come asap because I saw a UFO..
See Initials, Acronyms, and Abbreviations, 133-139

Building Sentences

A Crash Course in Sentence-building

In order to be a good sentence builder, you need to know your materials (the parts of speech) and their function (the parts of a sentence). Each of the parts of speech is covered in more detail later in this book, but this can help you get started.

Parts of Speech

Here is a sentence in which the parts of speech are labeled:

SEE ALSO
Parts of
Speech,
p. 25

Interjection   Article   Noun   Verb   Pronoun   Verb   Verb   Article   Noun

Hurray! The principal said she may close the school

Conjunction   Adverb   Adjective   Noun   Verb   Adjective   Preposition   Article   Noun

because so many students are sick with the flu.

The Parts of a Sentence

SEE ALSO
More About
Subjects
and
Predicates,
pp. 11-13
Nouns,
pp. 27-40
Pronouns,
pp. 41-52

▶ A **sentence** expresses a complete thought. It has a **subject** and a **predicate**.

▶ **Subjects** are nouns, pronouns, or phrases used as **nouns**. They tell what the sentence is about — a person, thing, or idea. For example,

The principal said she may close the school.

▶ The **predicate** tells about the subject, what the subject does or did, is or was. For example,

> The principal **closed the school because so many students are sick with the flu.**

▶ A **clause** is a group of words that has a subject and a predicate.

▶ A **main clause** can stand alone as a sentence.

> **The principal closed the school.**

▶ A **subordinate clause** is used with the main clause to express a related idea.

> The principal closed the school **because so many students are sick with the flu.**

SEE ALSO
Subordinating
Conjunctions,
p. 79

▶ A **phrase** is a group of words that has no subject or predicate. It may be used as a noun, verb, adjective, or adverb. For example, this phrase is used as an adverb because it tells how the students are sick.

> The principal said she may close the school because so many students are sick **with the flu.**

More About Subjects and Predicates

Simple Subject

The **simple subject** is the main noun or pronoun that names the subject. It is usually one word. It tells who or what the sentence is about.

MORE

*The tall **girl** with the frizzy red hair came to my party.*

If the simple subject is a proper noun — someone's name or a place — it can sometimes be more than one word.

***Amelia Jenks Bloomer** was a famous American feminist in the 1800s.*

*The **Empire State Building** was once the world's tallest building.*

Complete Subject

The **complete subject** is the simple subject and all the words that go with it.

***The tall girl with the frizzy red hair** came to my party.*

Simple Predicate

The **simple predicate** is the verb in the complete predicate. It can be one, two, three, or four words long.

SEE ALSO
Commas,
p. 87

*The tall girl with the frizzy red hair **came** to my party.*

*The tall girl with the frizzy red hair **was coming** to my party.*

*The tall girl with the frizzy red hair **should have come** to my party.*

*The tall girl with the frizzy red hair **should have been invited** to my party.*

Complete Predicate

The **complete predicate** is everything in the sentence that is not the complete subject.

The tall girl with the frizzy red hair **came to my party.**

Compound Subject

A **compound subject** is two or more simple subjects joined by a conjunction (**and** or **or**).

The goat, the horse, and the cow broke through the fence.

**SEE ALSO
Coordinating
Conjunctions,
p. 78**

Compound Predicate

A **compound predicate** is two or more verbs (simple predicates) joined by a conjunction (**and, or,** or **but**).

The goat **broke through the fence and ran away.**

A sentence can have both a compound subject and a compound predicate.

The goat, the horse, and the cow broke through the fence and ran away.

Four Kinds of Sentences and What They Do

Declarative, Interrogative, Imperative, and Exclamatory

People write and speak more declarative sentences than any other kind.

One way to group sentences is by what they do: they make statements or requests, ask questions, or exclaim strong feelings.

▸ Declarative Sentences (statements)

A **declarative sentence** makes a statement.

Thursday is my gerbil's birthday.

There will be a grammar test tomorrow.

**SEE ALSO
Periods,
Question
Marks,
p. 92**

2▸ Interrogative Sentences (questions)

An **interrogative sentence** asks a question.

Is this a picture of you when you were a baby?

Why do things like this always happen to me?

You can usually identify a question because the main verb comes before the subject.

**SEE ALSO
What is a
main verb?
p. 54**

3▸ Imperative Sentences (requests and commands)

An **imperative sentence** makes a request or gives a command.

Open your test booklets now.

Put that chicken down, or else!

Run!

You (Understood)

At first, you may think that an imperative sentence doesn't have a subject. But it does.

The subject of all imperative sentences is **you** because the speaker or writer is always giving you an order or asking you for a favor. But the word **you** is not usually spoken or written in the sentence. We say that the subject of the sentence is **you** (**understood**). That's because the listener or reader understands that the word **you** is the subject even though **you** isn't there.

(You) Put that chicken down, or else!

(You) Run!

▶ Exclamatory Sentences (exclamations)

An **exclamatory sentence** expresses strong feelings or emotions.

SEE ALSO
Exclamation
Points,
pp. 89-90

I got the highest grade on the math test!

My sister's cat had eight kittens!

I quit!

Three Ways to Build a Sentence

In English there are three basic sentence structures: simple, compound, and complex.

▶ 1 Simple Sentences

SEE ALSO
Subjects and
Predicates,
pp. 11-13

A **simple sentence** is made up of one complete subject and one complete predicate. A simple sentence can be short or long.

> She ate.

> My grandmother's neighbor from across the hallway ate a whole pot of spaghetti and meatballs by herself!

The sentence is still simple even if the subject or the predicate is a compound.

> Mom and Dad sang and danced.

▶ 2 Compound Sentences

SEE ALSO
Commas,
p. 85

A **compound sentence** is made up of two or more independent clauses (simple sentences). These independent clauses are joined by a comma and a conjunction.

> She asked me to the dance, and I said yes.

> You eat this banana and peanut butter sandwich, or I'll never make you lunch again.

Conjunctions that join independent clauses are called **coordinating conjunctions.** The three that are used most often are **and, or,** and **but.**

SEE ALSO Coordinating Conjunctions, p. 78

Sometimes you can use a semicolon to join independent clauses instead of a comma and a conjunction.

The mechanical dinosaur in the museum had a short circuit; it started to dance!

3▶ Complex Sentences

A **complex sentence** contains an independent clause and a dependent clause. The two clauses are joined by a subordinating conjunction.

SEE ALSO Subordinating Conjunctions, p. 79

We'll just have to wait here until the spaceship comes.

Whenever I see that monkey, I think of my counselor at camp.

Notice that in the last sentence above, the dependent clause (the one that begins with the subordinating conjunction **whenever**) comes at the beginning of the sentence. In a complex sentence it doesn't matter which comes first, the independent or dependent clause. That sentence could have been written

I think of my counselor at camp whenever I see that monkey.

When a Group of Words Is Not a Sentence

Fragments

A **fragment** is not quite a whole sentence because it is missing either the subject or the main verb. Even if the group of words begins with a capital letter and has a punctuation mark at the end, it is still a fragment if either the subject or the main verb is missing.

Slipping down the muddy bank and plopping into the river.

Who is slipping and plopping? The subject is missing.

Belinda, who came all the way from South Africa by plane.

What about her? What did she do? The predicate is missing.

How to Fix Fragments

Put in the missing subject or predicate so that the sentence makes complete sense, or take out a word that is keeping it from being a complete sentence.

A hippo in a tutu was slipping on the muddy bank and plopping into the river.

Belinda came all the way from South Africa by plane.

Belinda, who came all the way from South Africa by plane, had never seen snow before.

Run-ons

A **run-on sentence** is really two or more sentences (or independent clauses) that run together without the proper punctuation to join them.

It may rain today take your umbrella.

At first that may look like one sentence, but it's really two independent clauses with no punctuation to join them together.

How to Fix a Run-on Sentence

First, decide what the separate sentences are. Where does the first sentence end, and where does the second sentence begin?

It may rain today   take your umbrella

Then fix the run-on sentence in one of three ways:

1. Join the two sentences with a comma and a conjunction.

It may rain today, so take your umbrella.

(A comma by itself is not strong enough to join the two parts together. You must use both a comma and a conjunction.)

SEE ALSO
Commas,
p. 85
Semicolons,
pp. 95-96

2. Join the two sentences with a semicolon.

It may rain today; take your umbrella.

3. Make two separate sentences.

It may rain today. Take your umbrella.

Making Subjects and Verbs Work Together: Subject-Verb Agreement

SEE ALSO
Singular and Plural Nouns, pp. 28-31
First, Second, and Third Person Pronouns, p. 48

The **subject** and **verb** in a sentence must be the same (agree) in person (1st, 2nd, or 3rd) and in number (singular or plural).

▶ A **first person** subject takes a first person verb.

I am the cheese.

▶ A **second person** subject takes a second person verb.

You are going to get into trouble for this.

▶ A **third person** subject takes a third person verb.

Marilyn is not allowed to stay up that late.

▶ A **singular** subject takes a singular verb.

The porcupine sneezes.

▶ A **plural** subject takes a plural verb.

The porcupines sneeze.

TIP

In most cases your ear can be the judge of whether or not the subject and verb match up.

Subject and verb do not agree:
We has never been here before.

Subject and verb agree:
We have never been here before.

Subject-Verb Agreement Example: To Run

Here is the verb **to run** matched up with all the personal pronoun subjects to show how a subject and a verb agree (are the same) in person and number.

Singular

1st person: I run, am running, was running, do run, did run, etc.

2nd person: you run, are running, were running, do run, did run, etc.

3rd person: he, she, it runs, is running, was running, does run, did run, etc.

Plural

1st person: We run, are running, were running, do run, did run, etc.

2nd person: you run, are running, were running, do run, did run, etc.

3rd person: they run, are running, were running, do run, did run, etc.

Verbs with Collective Nouns

A **collective noun** is usually followed by a **singular verb** because the group usually acts together as a single unit.

My class has seen this movie.

SEE ALSO
Collective
Nouns,
p. 33

The **flock** of geese **flies** south every winter.

This **set** of tapes **is** on sale this week.

But sometimes a collective noun can be plural. That happens when members of the group are acting as separate individuals, not as a single unit.

Singular: The team is coming onto the field now.

Plural: The team are unable to make up their minds.

In the first sentence above, the people on the team are all doing the same thing together, so the collective noun (**team**) is singular and is followed by a singular verb (**is coming**).

In the second sentence above, the individual members of the team are not all acting together. **Team** here means separate people, not a single unit. That's why **team** takes a plural verb (**are**).

Verbs with Compound Subjects Joined by *And*

SEE ALSO
Compound
Subject,
p. 13

Compound subjects are plural when they are joined by **and**.

The duck and the goose were splashing in the pond.

Sometimes we use two food words together so often that we think of them as one dish.

EXCEPTION

peanut butter and jelly   bacon and eggs

When words like these are the subjects of a sentence, make the verb singular.

Macaroni and cheese is my favorite lunch.

Bread and water was all the prisoner got to eat.

Verbs with Compound Subjects Joined by *Or*

When **compound subjects** are joined by **or**, the verb matches the subject that follows **or**. That subject could be singular or plural.

Here is an easy way for you to decide whether the verb should be singular or plural. Leave out all the rest of the words in the sentence except the subject after **or** and the verb. If they sound right together, put the rest of the words back.

Either my dog or I am responsible for this accident.
(**CHECK:** I am responsible...)

Either you or your dog is responsible for this accident.
(**CHECK:** Your dog is responsible...)

Either she or her dogs are responsible for this accident.
(**CHECK:** Her dogs are responsible...)

Indefinite Pronouns: Singular or Plural

Some **indefinite pronouns** are singular. Some are plural. A few are both!

SEE ALSO
Indefinite
Pronouns,
pp. 49-50

Singular:

another	everybody	no one
anybody	everyone	nothing
anyone	everything	one
anything	much	somebody
each	neither	someone
either	nobody	something

Each (one) of the animals **makes** a different sound.
Neither (one) of his parents **is coming** to the game.

Plural:

both   few   many   others   several

Both are rock stars.
Many have known this weird story.

Either singular or plural:

all   any   most   none   some

These pronouns are plural when they refer to nouns (or pronouns) that can be counted one by one. They are singular when they refer to nouns (or pronouns) that cannot be counted.

Singular:
All of his **allowance was** spent on junk.
Plural:
All of his **clothes were** in the laundry.

Singular:
Some of this **book is** boring.
Plural:
Some of these **books are** from the library.

Singular:
Most of the **video was** out of focus.
Plural:
Most of the **nuts were** eaten by the monkey.

Parts of Speech

The eight parts of speech are the building blocks of sentences. When you learn to use the parts of speech correctly, your sentences will mean just what you want them to mean.

Adjectives

Adverbs

Prepositions

Conjunctions

Interjections

Nouns

What is a noun?

A **noun** is a word that names a person, animal, place, thing, or idea. There are more nouns in the English language than any other kind of word.

Persons	Animals	Places	Things	Ideas
teacher	shark	school	pen	concentration
student	hamster	gym	computer	wisdom
girl	fish	Lake Erie	mailbox	kindness
boy	aardvark	Chicago	skateboard	freedom
Mrs. Li	bear	village	tree	fear
Tanya	flea	Africa	cereal	love

A, an, and the are special words called **articles**. They are noun signals. They can often tip you off that there's a **noun** coming up in the sentence.

MORE

The noun could be the very next word after the article.

A *clown* ate *the apple*.

Or it could be one or more words later.

A *roly-poly, floppy-eared, hilariously funny* clown ate *the* big, red, delicious apple.

Kinds of Nouns

Singular and Plural Nouns

Singular means one of something. **Plural** means more than one.

Five Ways to Make Nouns Plural

▶ You can make most nouns plural by just adding **s**.

one pencil	four pencil**s**
one car	a garage full of car**s**

▶ If the noun ends with **s**, **ch**, **sh**, **x**, or **z**, add **es** to make it plural.

one dress	a rack of dress**es**
one church	three church**es**
one brush	a box of brush**es**
one fox	a den of fox**es**
one buzz	many buzz**es** of many bees

3▶ To make some nouns that end with **f** or **fe** plural, change the **f** to **v** and add **es**.

knife	knives
half	halves
leaf	leaves

 Not all nouns that end with **f** or **fe** follow this rule. For example, **safe**, **waif**, and **bluff** don't. But most do.

4▶ Add **s** if the letter in front of the **y** is a vowel, to make plural a noun that ends in **y**.

toy	toys
key	keys

5▶ Drop the **y** and add **ies** if the letter in front of the **y** is a consonant.

dictionary	dictionaries
penny	pennies

Some nouns have tricky plurals.

one man	a group of men

Forty-One Irregular Plurals

Some nouns are not regular. When irregular nouns become plural, they change their spellings, or they stay the same, and a few even have more than one plural form. Here are forty-one of the trickiest irregular nouns with their plural forms.

Singular	Plural
alga	algae
alumna	alumnae
alumnus	alumni
antenna (on a television)	antennas
antenna (on a bug's head)	antennae
appendix	appendixes, appendices
bacterium	bacteria
bison	bison
buffalo	buffalos, buffaloes, buffalo
bus	buses, busses
cactus	cacti, cactuses
child	children
corps	corps
crisis	crises
datum	data
deer	deer
die	dice
dwarf	dwarfs, dwarves
foot	feet
fish	fish, fishes
goose	geese
half	halves
hippopotamus	hippopotami, hippopotamuses

hoof	hoofs, hooves
louse	lice
man	men
moose	moose
mouse	mice
octopus	octopi, octopuses, octopodes
ox	oxen
scarf	scarves, scarfs
series	series
sheep	sheep
staff (stick or line for charting music)	staves
staff (group of workers)	staffs
stegosaurus	stegosauri
swine	swine
talisman	talismans
tooth	teeth
wharf	wharfs, wharves
woman	women

Common and Proper Nouns

▶ A **common noun** names any old, regular, ordinary person, animal, place, thing, or idea. Nothing specific.

▶ A **proper noun** names a very specific, very particular person, animal, place, thing, or idea.

▶ A **proper noun** always begins with a capital letter.

Common Nouns	Proper Nouns
woman	Harriet Tubman
boy	Aaron Leong
superhero	Batman
dog	Lassie
horse	Black Beauty
cat	Cheshire Cat
mountain	Mount Everest
river	Mississippi River
city	Boston
building	Astrodome
school	Columbia Middle School
house	Monticello
holiday	Fourth of July

Concrete and Abstract Nouns

▶ A **concrete noun** names a person, animal, place, or thing that you can actually see, touch, taste, hear, or smell.

radio spaghetti tuba onions fire muffins perfume cloud

▶ An **abstract noun** names an idea, feeling, emotion, or quality.

beauty   happiness   ability   anger   nature   love   speed

These things exist, but you cannot actually pick them up, hear them, taste them, smell them, or even see them in the real world. (You can see that someone is angry. You might be able to see what makes her angry. But you can't really see anger.)

Collective Nouns

A **collective noun** names a group of people, animals, or things. Here are some examples:

People		
audience	crew	cast
crowd	family	band
gang	group	choir
jury	chorus	nation
class	orchestra	quartet
club	quintet	committee
trio	duo	staff

Animals		
flock	herd	swarm
pack	brood	team
gaggle	colony	warren
school	pride	litter

Things		
bunch	set	cache
bundle	stack	batch
fleet	cluster	bouquet
pod	clump	clutch

SEE ALSO
Verbs with
Collective
Nouns,
pp. 21-22

Compound Nouns

A **compound noun** is made up of two or more words used together.

SEE ALSO
Building
Compound
Words,
pp. 129-130

Compound nouns can be

One Word	Two Words	Hyphenated
shoelace	seat belt	baby-sitter
flashlight	high school	editor-in-chief
applesauce	word processor	great-grandchild

If you can't remember if a compound noun is one word, two words, or hyphenated, check your dictionary.

Eight Uses of Nouns

▶ **Subject of the Sentence**

The **subject** is the person, animal, place, thing, or idea that the sentence is about.

One way to find the subject is to ask yourself who or what is performing the action of the verb.

The **teacher** laughed hysterically.

What person is that sentence about? The teacher. Who laughed? The teacher. **Teacher** is the subject of the sentence.

Pencils always break just before a big test.

What things is that sentence about? Pencils. What things always break? Pencils. **Pencils** is the subject of the sentence.

Enthusiasm can be the difference between winning and losing.

SEE ALSO
Subjects and Predicates, pp. 11-13

What idea is that sentence about? Enthusiasm. What idea can be the difference? Enthusiasm. **Enthusiasm** is the subject of the sentence.

2 ▸ Predicate Noun (or Predicate Nominative)

A **predicate noun** comes after the verb **to be** and means the same thing as the subject of the sentence.

(A predicate noun can also come after a linking verb: **to become, to remain,** etc.)

My brother is the funniest **kid** in the world.

Lorraine will become **chairperson** of the committee.

I am the **boss**, and don't you forget it!

How to Identify a Predicate Noun

You can check to see if a word is a predicate noun by switching it with the subject. If the sentence still makes sense, that word is the predicate noun.

Ms. Youngman is the substitute math teacher today.

The substitute math teacher today is Ms. Youngman.

Ms. Youngman = teacher; teacher = Ms. Youngman. **Teacher** is the predicate noun in the first sentence above. **Ms. Youngman** is the predicate noun in the second sentence.

3 ▸ Appositive

An **appositive** is a word or phrase (group of words) that comes after another word, and identifies, explains, or gives information about that word. The appositive word or phrase is set off from the rest of the sentence by one or two commas.

*Tokyo, **the capital of Japan**, is a crowded city.*

*Give this robot dog to that tall woman, **one of our secret agents**.*

*The school janitor, **Mr. Forest**, turned on the radiators.*

When one noun is the appositive for another noun, we sometimes say that they are "in apposition."

4 Direct Object of a Verb

The **direct object** is the person, animal, place, thing, or idea that receives the action of the verb.

> Carlos locked the **coach** in the gym.

What's the action? Locking someone in. What person got locked in? The coach. **Coach** is the direct object of the verb.

> From the top of the skyscraper, Maria can hardly see the **street**.

What's the action? Seeing something. What place can Maria hardly see? The street. **Street** is the direct object of the verb.

> Superheroes fight **injustice** wherever they go.

What's the action? Fighting an idea. What idea do superheroes fight? Injustice. **Injustice** is the direct object of the verb.

5 Indirect Object of a Verb

The **indirect object** receives the action of the verb — indirectly.

> Should I send **David** some extra money?

What am I sending? Some extra money. Who will receive the extra money (if I send it)? David. **David** is the indirect object.

Ways to Identify the Indirect Object

1. Imagine that **to** or **for** is in front of the indirect object.

   Should I send (to) David some extra money?

2. The indirect object always comes before the direct object. In the example above, **some extra money** is the direct object of the verb **should send**.

3. Some verbs are usually followed by indirect objects: **give, buy, throw, show, award, lend, save, bake, send,** and **knit**.

   Paloma tried to give (to) her teacher the message.
   Karen baked (for) Mrs. Freedman a carrot-raisin cake.
   Save (for) me a seat at the Killer Kanary concert.

6 ▸ Object of the Preposition

SEE ALSO
Prepositions
pp. 74-77

A **preposition** is a word that shows location, movement, or direction. Some common prepositions are **in, on, with, by, for,** and **under**.

A preposition is always followed by a noun (or pronoun) called the **object of the preposition**. Together, with the preposition, they form a **prepositional phrase**.

against the stormy **sea**

beneath a pile of dinosaur **bones**

during the **Revolutionary War**

into the raging **volcano**

under the **table**

SEE ALSO
Prepositional
Phrases
p. 77

7 ▸ Object Complement

An **object complement** is a word that completes the meaning of the direct object. **Complement** comes from the verb **to complete.** You use an object complement when the direct object wouldn't make complete sense by itself.

My grandfather named his cat **Peaches**.

The country elected Lincoln **president**.

Peaches and **president** are object complements. Without those words, you wouldn't know what name my grandfather gave to his cat or to what office Lincoln was elected.

8 ▸ To Show Possession

A **possessive noun** tells who or what owns (possesses) something.

The **boy**'s hat is on the floor.

MORE

Who owns the hat? The boy does. **Boy's** is a possessive noun.

Alaska's *weather is much milder in the summer.*

What place's weather is milder in the summer? Alaska's is.
Alaska's is a possessive noun.

How to Make Nouns Possessive

To make a singular noun possessive, just add 's.

president	the president's plane
ox	the ox's tale
boss	my boss's car
Holmes	Sherlock Holmes's violin

To make a plural noun possessive, check the last letter of the plural noun. If it's an **s**, just add an apostrophe.

girls	those girls' science kits
students	the students' bookbags
gerbils	my gerbils' food

If the last letter of the plural noun is not **s**, add 's.

men	the men's shoes
mice	her mice's cheese
teeth	your teeth's enamel

SEE ALSO
Apostrophes,
p. 84

If you know the ways nouns are used, you are less
likely to make a mistake using a pronoun.

Pronouns

What is a pronoun?

A **pronoun** is a word that takes the place of a noun. Almost anything a noun can do, a pronoun can do, too. Pronouns are handy little words because when you use them, you don't have to keep repeating nouns all the time.

Without pronouns:

> Jennifer said that Jennifer was going to give Jennifer's cats Jennifer's cats' food.

With pronouns:

> Jennifer said that **she** was going to give **her** cats **their** food.

There are six kinds of pronouns: personal, demonstrative, indefinite, intensive, reflexive, and interrogative, but personal pronouns are the one we use most.

SEE ALSO
Five Other Kinds of Pronouns, pp. 49-51

Personal Pronouns

Personal pronouns refer to specific people and things. In order to use personal pronouns, it is important to know about **case** (subject, object, and possessive), **number** (singular or plural), and **person** (first, second, or third).

Subject, Object, and Possessive Cases

Knowing how a pronoun is used in a sentence helps you to know what form to use.

▶ Subject Pronouns

I, *you*, *he*, *she*, *it*, *we*, *they*

A **subject pronoun** is used as a subject or a predicate noun.

*I am the lion tamer, and **you** are just the lion.*

*It was **she** who did that.*

▶ Object Pronouns

me*, *you*, *him*, *her*, *it*, *us*, *them

SEE ALSO
Eight Uses of Nouns, pp. 34-40

An **object pronoun** is used as an indirect object, direct object, or object of a preposition.

*Dad told **me** to give **him** the cake.*

*The boys are going with **us** and **them**.*

*The teacher saw **you** do **it**.*

Pronouns come in subject/object pairs:

Subject	Object
I	me
you	you
he	him
she	her
it	it
we	us
they	them

3 ▶ Possessive Pronouns

Possessive pronouns take the place of possessive nouns (nouns that show ownership).

> **Her** sandwich is much thicker than **his.**

> Lola's sandwich is much thicker than Larry's.

SEE ALSO
Eight Uses of Nouns:
To Show Possession,
pp. 39-40
Note on its and it's,
p. 127

Possessive Pronouns	
my	mine
your	yours
his	
her	hers
its	
our	ours
their	theirs

Never put a noun right after **mine, yours, hers, ours,** and **theirs** because, by themselves, they take the place of possessive nouns.

> If this thing isn't **hers,** it must be **theirs.**

> **Yours** is much funnier-looking than **mine.**

Seven Uses of Personal Pronouns

Pronouns are used to replace nouns in the following ways:

▶ **1** **Subject of a sentence:**

> The boy ran for the school bus.
>
> **He** ran for the school bus.

▶ **2** **Predicate pronouns:**

> The leader of the troop is Dave.
>
> The leader of the troop is **he**.

▶ **3** **Direct object of a verb:**

> I saw Karen at the mall.
>
> I saw **her** at the mall.

**SEE ALSO
Eight Uses of
Nouns,
pp. 34-40**

▶ **4** **Indirect object of a verb:**

> Try to sell Mr. and Mrs. Cejwin a glass of lemonade.
>
> Try to sell **them** a glass of lemonade.

▶ **5** **Object of a preposition:**

> The truckload of feathers fell on the two monkeys
>
> The truckload of feathers fell on **them**.

> **1** and **2** use subject pronouns.
>
> **3** , **4** , and **5** use object pronouns.

6 Appositive:

> The new students, Tim and **she**, were asked to stand.
>
> Please take the advice of your friends, Jane and **me**.

7 To show possession (ownership):

> This is Mary, Paula, and Sybil's science project.
>
> This is **their** science project.

SEE ALSO
Eight Uses
of Nouns
pp. 34-40
Note on its
and it's,
p. 127

How to Choose the Correct Pronoun: Subject or Object?

Sometimes people don't know whether to use the subject or the object pronoun in sentences like these:

> My brother and (I, me) went to the pet store.

Here the pronoun is a part of the subject, so use a subject pronoun.

> My brother and I went to the pet store.

> The principal saw Tamika and (I, me).

Here the pronoun is a direct object, so use an object pronoun.

> The principal saw Tamika and **me**.

And remember, always put yourself last.
Grammar is polite.

MORE ➡

Quick Clue

Here's another way to pick the right pronoun. Take away the other words that go with **I** or **me**.

Me went to the pet store.

You can usually hear which pronoun is the right one. Now put the other words back.

My brother and **I** went to the pet store.

Try it with the other sample sentence below.

The principal saw Tamika and (I, me).
The principal saw I.
The principal saw me.
The principal saw Tamika and **me**.

This method works with all the other subject and object personal pronouns, too. Check it out.

How to Decide Between Who and Whom

Many people mix up **who** and **whom**.
Who is a subject pronoun. When a sentence (or clause) needs a subject or a predicate nominative, use **who**.

Who will be watching?
The president of the United States is who?
I recognized the girl who was ice skating.

Whom is an object pronoun. When a sentence needs a direct object, indirect object, or object of a preposition, use **whom**.

SEE ALSO
Subject,
Object, and
Possessive
Cases,
p. 42

Direct object: Whom did you invite to the party?
Indirect Object: You knitted whom a cashmere sweater?
Object of the preposition: To whom did you give the ring?

If you really get confused about using **who** and **whom**, try this. In your mind, rewrite just the part of the sentence that contains **who** or **whom**. Instead of **who**, use **he**. Instead of **whom**, use **him**. See which one sounds better. If **him** sounds better, use **whom** in the original sentence. Otherwise, use **who**.

> *The boy (who, whom) we chose class president moved to Ohio.*

Try saying: We chose he. We chose him. **Him** sounds better, so it's:

> *The boy whom we chose class president moved to Ohio.*

> *That is the boy (who, whom) is moving to Ohio.*

Try saying: He is moving. Him is moving. **He** sounds right, so it's:

> *That is the boy who is moving to Ohio.*

Number

The "number" of a pronoun shows whether the pronoun refers to a single person or thing (singular) or more than one person or thing (plural). Number is important because it tells you what verb to use — singular or plural.

Singular pronouns are **I, me, my, mine, he, she, him, her, his, hers, it,** and **its**.

Plural pronouns are **we, us, our, ours, they, them, their,** and **theirs**.

You and **yours** are both singular and plural.

First Person, Second Person, and Third Person Pronouns

We also divide personal pronouns into three groups called **persons.**

▶ **First person** is the person speaking:

I, we
me, us
my, mine, our, ours

▶ **Second person** is the person spoken to: *you, your, yours*

▶ **Third person** is the person or thing spoken about:

he, she, it
his, her, hers, its
him, her, it
they, them, their, theirs

Here is a chart that shows the personal pronouns by case, number and person:

		Singular	Plural
1st person	**subject**	I	we
	object	me	us
	possessive	my, mine	our, ours
2nd person	**subject**	you	you
	object	you	you
	possessive	your, yours	your, yours
3rd person	**subject**	he, she, it	they
	object	him, her, it	them
	possessive	his, her, hers, its	their, theirs

Five Other Kinds of Pronouns

▶ Demonstrative Pronouns

Demonstrative pronouns point out (demonstrate) specific persons, animals, places, things, and ideas. There are only four of them.

this	that	these	those

Please exchange **this** for **that** and **these** for **those**.

This is the way to dress the baby for warm weather.

2 Indefinite Pronouns

Indefinite pronouns refer to nouns in a general, indefinite sort of way. Here's a list of words that can be used as indefinite pronouns.

all	another	any	anybody	anyone	anything
both	each	either	everybody	everyone	everything
few	many	neither	nobody	no one	nothing
one	others	several	some	somebody	someone
			something		

Everybody can do **something**, but **nobody** can do **everything**!

Many bought tickets to the show, but **few** actually came.

SEE ALSO
Demonstrative
Adjectives,
pp. 64-65

Some indefinite pronouns can also be used as **adjectives** (for example: **all, any, both, each, few, one, several,** and **some**). When these words are adjectives, they have nouns after them (**both** cats, **few** people, etc.) When they are indefinite pronouns, they have no nouns after them. (**Each** has his own book. **Both** knew the answer.)

❸ Intensive Pronouns

Intensive pronouns emphasize (intensify) a noun or another pronoun. They really make you notice the nouns and pronouns they go with.

Singular	Plural
myself	ourselves
yourself	yourselves
himself	
herself	themselves
itself	

Kareem **himself** ordered the birthday cake.

Roxy went right up to the mayor **herself** and said, "Hi!"

◢ Reflexive Pronouns

The very same pronouns that we call intensive pronouns can also be used as **reflexive pronouns.** They don't intensify; they refer back to (reflect) the subject of the sentence.

Fatima wanted to kick **herself** when she saw her mistake.

You'll have to ask **yourself** what you really want to do.

◢ Interrogative Pronouns

Interrogative pronouns ask questions. There are only five of them.

what	which	who	whom	whose

I demand to know **who** did **what** to **whom!**

Which should I leave, and **whose** should I take?

Master List of all Pronouns

Here are all the pronouns — personal, demonstrative, indefinite, intensive, interrogative, and reflexive — in alphabetical order for easy reference:

all	its	something
another	itself	that
any	many	their
anybody	me	theirs
anyone	mine	them
anything	my	themselves
both	myself	these
each	neither	they
either	nobody	this
everybody	none	those
everyone	no one	us
everything	nothing	we
few	one	what
he	others	which
her	our	who
hers	ours	whom
herself	ourselves	whose
him	several	you
himself	she	your
his	some	yours
I	somebody	yourself
it	someone	yourselves

Verbs

What is a verb?

A **verb** is a word that shows action or being. Whatever you're doing can be expressed by a verb.

Without a verb, a group of words cannot be a sentence. A sentence can be as short as one word long, as long as that one word is a verb. **Go!**, **Stop!**, and **Eat!** are all perfectly good one-word sentences. (If you're wondering what the subjects of those sentences are, see **You Understood** on page 15.)

Verbs That Show Action

Action doesn't mean just physical action like to **jump, run, throw, scream, swim,** and **climb.** Action also means quiet, slow, peaceful actions, both physical and mental, like to **think, listen, sleep, read, look, breathe, hear, wonder,** and **dream.**

Main Verbs and Helping Verbs

What is a main verb?

The **main verb** expresses the main action or state of being in the sentence.

> The principal **called** Julio into his office.
>
> Julio **is** nervous.

What is a helping verb?

Helping verbs are nice and help the main verb express tenses. There are twenty-three of these verbs.

> am, are, is, was, were, be, being, been
>
> do, does, did
>
> have, has, had
>
> may, must, might
>
> can, could, would, should
>
> shall, will

A main verb can have up to three helping verbs.

Rozzie **was** laughing so hard, she spilled her soda.

Jose **should have** known the answer to the math question.

Kim **will have been** waiting an hour by the time we get there.

Notice that the verb **to be** can be a helping verb or a main verb, or even both in the same sentence. (What a verb!)

SEE ALSO
To Be,
pp. 60-62

As the **main verb**:	*We are so glad that you will be there.*
As a **helping verb**:	*I am leaving this house this minute!*
As a **helping verb** and a **main verb**:	*Miguel was being bad again.*

Verb Tenses

Tense means **time** in grammar. The **tense** of a verb tells you when the action of the verb takes place. There are six main tenses.

▶ **1** **Present tense** means now:

I **ride** *my bike this very minute.*

▶ **2** **Past tense** means before now — a second or a million years ago:

I **rode** *my horse the day before yesterday.*

▶ **3** **Future tense** means not yet (but any time after now):

I **will ride** *my skateboard to school this morning.*

▶ **4** **Present perfect tense** means started in the past and just recently finished or still going on:

I **have ridden** *my moped around the park three times (and I'm still riding it).*

MORE ➡

In grammar, **perfect** means completed or finished.

5▷ **Past perfect tense** means finished before some other past action:

*I **had ridden** my wagon for a mile before I fell off.*

6▷ **Future perfect tense** means the action will be started and finished in the future:

*I **will have ridden** the camel for hours before I get there.*

The Three Principal Parts of Verbs: Present, Past, and Past Participle

Every verb has three main parts called **principal parts.**

1▷ The **present** is used by itself for the present tense (I go) and with the helping verb **will** for the future tense (I will go).

2▷ The **past** is used for the past tense (I went).

3▷ The **past participle** is used with the helping verbs **have, has,** or **had** to form the three perfect tenses:

> **present perfect** (I have gone)
>
> **past perfect** (I had gone)
>
> **future perfect** (I will have gone)

Regular Verbs

Most verbs are regular. **Regular verbs** just add **d** or **ed** when they change principal parts from the present to the past to the past participle.

Present	Past	Past Participle (used with have, has, had)
Now I jump.	Yesterday I jumped.	I have jumped.
Now we skate.	Yesterday we skated.	We had skated.

Ninety Irregular Verbs

Irregular verbs form their past tenses and past participles in other unpredictable ways. Here are ninety of the most common of these tricky irregular verbs:

Present (Now I...)	Past (Yesterday I...)	Past Participle (I have or had...)
arise	arose	arisen
awake	awoke or awaked	awaked or awoke
bear	bore	borne
beat	beat	beaten
begin	began	begun
bind	bound	bound
bite	bit	bitten or bit
blow	blew	blown
break	broke	broken
bring	brought	brought
burst	burst	burst
buy	bought	bought
catch	caught	caught
choose	chose	chosen
cling	clung	clung
come	came	come

cut	cut	cut
deal	dealt	dealt
dive	dived or dove	dived
do	did	done
draw	drew	drawn
drink	drank	drunk
drive	drove	driven
eat	ate	eaten
fall	fell	fallen
fight	fought	fought
flee	fled	fled
fling	flung	flung
fly	flew	flown
forbid	forbade or forbad	forbidden
forget	forgot	forgotten or forgot
freeze	froze	frozen
get	got	got, gotten
give	gave	given
go	went	gone
grow	grew	grown
hang (a picture)	hung	hung
hang (a person)	hanged	hanged
hide	hid	hidden or hid
hold	held	held
keep	kept	kept
know	knew	known
lay	laid	laid
leave	left	left
lend	lent	lent
lie	lay	lain
lose	lost	lost
meet	met	met

pay	paid	paid
read	read	read
rid	rid	rid
ride	rode	ridden
ring	rang	rung
rise	rose	risen
run	ran	run
say	said	said
see	saw	seen
set	set	set
shake	shook	shaken
shine (the sun)	shone	shone
shoot	shot	shot
show	showed	shown or showed
shrink	shrank or shrunk	shrunk
sing	sang	sung
sit	sat	sat
slay	slew	slain
slide	slid	slid
speak	spoke	spoken
spin	spun	spun
spring	sprang	sprung
stand	stood	stood
steal	stole	stolen
sting	stung	stung
stride	strode	stridden
strike	struck	struck
strive	strove	striven
swear	swore	sworn
swim	swam	swum
swing	swung	swung
take	took	taken

teach	taught	taught
tear	tore	torn
tell	told	told
think	thought	thought
throw	threw	thrown
wake	waked or woke	waked or woken
wear	wore	worn
wring	wrung	wrung
write	wrote	written

If a verb has more than one choice for a principal part (for example, **waked** or **woken**), you can use whichever one sounds better to you.

The Verb "To Be" and Other Linking Verbs

The main verb preceded by to is called the infinitive.

A **linking verb** links the subject to other words in the sentence. Linking verbs do not show action. They just say that someone or something is, was, or will be.

To Be

The verb **to be** (sometimes called "the verb of being") is the most common, most popular, most used verb in the English language. You use this verb dozens of times every day without realizing it.

There are only eight words to the verb **to be:**

am   are   is   was   were   be   being   been

The six tenses of the ever-popular verb **to be:**

Singular	**Plural**
Present Tense	
I am	we are
you are	you are
he, she, it is	they are
Past Tense	
I was	we were
you were	you were
he, she, it was	they were
Future Tense	
I will be	we will be
you will be	you will be
he, she, it will be	they will be
Present Perfect Tense	
I have been	we have been
you have been	you have been
he, she, it has been	they have been

SEE ALSO
Subject-Verb Agreement, pp. 20-21

MORE ➡

Past Perfect Tense

I had been   we had been
you had been   you had been
he, she, it had been   they had been

Future Perfect Tense

I will have been   we will have been
you will have been   you will have been
he, she, it will
    have been   they will have been

Linking Verbs

Here is a list of the most common **linking verbs** except for **to be.**

SEE ALSO
Predicate
Nouns,
pp. 35-36
Predicate
Adjectives,
p. 68

| to seem | to appear | to look | to sound | to feel |
| to taste | to grow | to remain | to smell | to become |

Linking verbs are never followed by direct objects. They are followed by nouns (called **predicate nouns**) or adjectives (called **predicate adjectives**).

▶ Linking verbs followed by predicate nouns:

With that one act, he **became** a **hero.**

She **remained** ping-pong **champ** for four years.

▶ Linking verbs followed by predicate adjectives:

Grandma **grows** more **beautiful** each day.

You **seem** awfully **quiet**. Do you **feel sick?**

▶ Sometimes a verb that is a linking verb in one sentence can be an action verb in another   When it is an action verb, it will be followed by a direct object, not a predicate adjective or predicate noun.

Linking verb: That doesn't **sound** right to me.

Action verb: **Sound** the fire alarm!

Linking verb: The stew **smells** delicious.

Action verb: Can you **smell** the garlic in this stew?

Linking verb: I think my soup **tastes** too salty.

Action verb: May I **taste** some Bubblegum Delight yogurt?

Linking verb: The teacher **looks** funny today, doesn't she?

Action verb: Come **look** at my hair-do!

Adjectives

What is an adjective?

An **adjective** is a word that tells us more about a noun or a pronoun. An adjective describes or modifies (limits the use of) a noun.

Adjectives Answer Three Questions

Adjectives usually answer three questions about the nouns they describe: 1) **what kind of?** 2) **how many?** 3) **which one?**

▶ What kind of?

> Roslyn spotted a **huge** monster in the cave!

What kind of monster? **Huge.**

▶ How many?

> **Six** ice cream cones, please.

How many cones? **Six.**

▶ Which one (or which ones)?

> I'll take **that** dress.

Which dress? **That** one.

Three Kinds of Adjectives

▶ **Demonstrative Adjectives**

This, that, these, and **those** are called **demonstrative adjectives.** They point out (demonstrate) nouns. They always answer the question **which one(s)?**

These cookies taste great, but I wouldn't eat **those** muffins.

Which cookies taste great? Which muffins should I not eat?

This, that, these, and **those** can also act as pronouns. Demonstrative pronouns are not followed by nouns as demonstrative adjectives are. They take the place of nouns.

SEE ALSO
Demonstrative
Pronouns,
p. 49

Demonstrative adjectives:

Give me **that** comic book, and
I'll give you **this** baseball card.

Demonstrative pronouns:

Give me **that**, and I'll give you **this**.

❷ Common Adjectives

A **common adjective**, like a common noun, is just a plain, ordinary, everyday adjective. It describes a noun in a general way. It is not capitalized (unless it's the first word in a sentence).

Here are some common examples of common adjectives:			
busy	bitter	soft	colorful
cooperative	warm	blue	sunny
red	juicy	grumpy	
invisible	wet	gross	

3 ▶ Proper Adjectives

A **proper adjective** is made from a proper noun. It is always capitalized.

Proper Noun	Proper Adjective
China	Chinese
Ireland	Irish
Switzerland	Swiss
Mars	Martian
Queen Elizabeth I	Elizabethan
U.S. Constitution	Constitutional

Sometimes a proper noun doesn't change at all to become a proper adjective. (Remember, a word is an adjective when it describes a noun.)

> She's a **Hollywood** actress with a **Texas** accent who loves **Idaho** potatoes, **New England** clam chowder, and **Maine** lobsters.

All proper nouns can be made into or used as proper adjectives.

Comparison of Adjectives: Positive, Comparative, and Superlative

Sometimes one person or thing is taller or bigger or faster than someone or something else. Sometimes one person or thing is the tallest or biggest or fastest of all. To show these comparisons, an adjective can be expressed three ways (called **degrees**).

Positive Degree (describing one)	Comparative Degree (comparing two)	Superlative Degree (comparing more than two)
great	greater	greatest
disgusting	more disgusting	most disgusting

How to Compare Adjectives

▶ Add **er** and **est** to short adjectives of one syllable (and sometimes two syllables).

short	shorter	shortest

▶ If a one- or two-syllable adjective ends with a consonant and **y**, change the **y** to **i**, then add **er** and **est**.

happy	happier	happiest
ugly	uglier	ugliest

▶ If a short adjective ends with **e**, just add **r** and **st**.

little	littler	littlest

▶ Put **more** and **most** in front of longer adjectives (two, three, or more syllables).

alert	more alert	most alert
beautiful	more beautiful	most beautiful
interesting	more interesting	most interesting

MORE ▶

Whether to add **er** and **est** or to use **more** and **most** can be tricky. In most cases, you can trust your ears. When in doubt, check your dictionary.

▶ Some adjectives are **irregular** and don't follow these rules.

good	better	best
bad	worse	worst
many	more	most

▶ Don't add **er** or **est** at the same time you use **more** or **most**. That's too much.

~~more smarter~~   ~~most popularest~~

Where an Adjective Goes in a Sentence

Usually an adjective comes in front of the noun it is describing.

The **gigantic** creature was hiding in the **scary** cave.

But an adjective can also come after a linking verb, like **to be**, and describe the subject of the sentence. Then it's called a **predicate adjective**.

The creature was **gigantic**.

**SEE ALSO
Linking
Verbs,
pp. 62-63**

Adverbs

What is an adverb?

An **adverb** is a word that tells us more about 1) a verb; 2) an adjective; or 3) another adverb.

We sometimes say that an adverb describes or modifies (limits the meaning of) these words.

When Adverbs Describe Verbs

Adverbs answer three questions about the verbs they describe: 1) **how?** 2) **when?** 3) **where?**

 How?

*The pig danced **terribly**.*

How did the pig dance? **Terribly.**

There are hundreds of adverbs that tell **how**. Here are some examples:

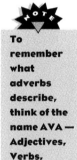

To remember what adverbs describe, think of the name AVA — Adjectives, Verbs, Adverbs.

Adverbs that tell *how:*			
badly	fast	stupidly	brilliantly
loudly	gracefully	cleverly	quietly
vigorously	eagerly	skillfully	well
easily	slowly	wildly	too

Where?

> The pig danced **here.**

Where did she dance? **Here.**

Some other adverbs that tell *where:*					
above	down	inside	anywhere	everywhere	outside
away	here	there	backward	near	up

Some of these adverbs that tell **where** can also be used as prepositions:

> **near** the boat
>
> **up** the stairs

SEE ALSO
Object of the
Preposition,
pp. 38-39
Prepositional
Phrases,
p. 77

 When?

> The pig danced **yesterday.**

When did she dance? **Yesterday.**

Some other adverbs that tell *when:*				
before	immediately	sometimes	daily	late
soon	periodically	lately	suddenly	eventually
never	then	finally	now	today
first	often	tomorrow	forever	seldom
tonight	frequently	yesterday	never	early

You can even put adverbs that answer different questions about the same verb together in one sentence.

The pig danced terribly here yesterday.

When Adverbs Describe Adjectives

Adverbs usually answer the question **how?** when they describe adjectives.

There are two adjectives in the sentences below, **ugly** and **old**.

Without adverbs: *My ugly dog likes old bones.*
With adverbs: *My **extremely** ugly dog likes **very** old bones.*

How ugly is my dog? **Extremely.** How old are the bones? **Very.**

Here are more examples of adverbs describing adjectives:			
really funny	quite lovely	historically important	fully aware
terribly bad	fairly heavy	somewhat depressed	too tall
rather sticky	amazingly good	annoyingly loud	not fair

When Adverbs Describe Other Adverbs

In the sentences below, **quickly** is an adverb. The words in italics (the slanted words) are also adverbs. They are modifying **quickly** and are answering the questions **how?** or, more exactly, **by how much?**

He eats quickly.

He eats *so* quickly.

He eats *too* quickly.

He eats *very* quickly.

He eats *quite* quickly.

He eats *rather* quickly.

He eats *really* quickly.

He eats *awfully* quickly.

He eats *somewhat* quickly.

He eats *extremely* quickly.

He eats *amazingly* quickly.

He eats *exceedingly* quickly.

He eats *extraordinarily* quickly.

(He's going to get sick *unbelievably* quickly!)

How to Change an Adjective into an Adverb

Many (but not all) adverbs end with the letters **ly**. You can often change an adjective into an adverb by adding **ly**.

soft + *ly* = soft**ly**   awful + *ly* = awful**ly**

The three most common adverbs used in English are not, very, and too.

Comparison of Adverbs: Positive, Comparative, and Superlative

Adverbs can be compared just like adjectives.

Positive Degree (to modify one word)	Comparative Degree (to compare two words)	Superlative Degree (to compare more than two)
soon	sooner	soonest
rapidly	more rapidly	most rapidly

Glenn walks rapidly. His father walks **more rapidly** (than Glenn does). His grandfather walks **most rapidly** of the three.

SEE ALSO
Comparison of
Adjectives,
pp. 66–68

Prepositions

What is a preposition?

A **preposition** is a word that shows the relationship of one word in a sentence to another word. The four things that prepositions tell are 1) **where something is** (location); 2) **where something is going** (direction); 3) **when something happens** (time); 4) the **relationship** between a noun or a pronoun and another word in a sentence.

Four Things Prepositions Tell

▶ Location

Many prepositions tell where something is in relation to something else.

> Amanda's guinea pig is **outside** its cage.

Other prepositions that show location are: **in, on, near, under,** and **inside.**

▶ Direction

Other prepositions tell where something is going.

> Amanda's guinea pig ran **to** her cage.

Other prepositions that tell direction are: **around, toward, through, past,** and **beside.**

▶ Time

A few prepositions help to tell time in a sentence.

> I'll wait **until** noon, and then I'm leaving.
>
> **During** the carnival, Simon lost his shoe.

▶ Relationship

Other prepositions show the relationships between a noun (or pronoun) and another word.

> Sasha went to the Halloween party **with** Shana.
>
> This exciting book was written **by** Mark Twain.

Master List of One-word Prepositions			
aboard	below	in	since
about	beneath	inside	through
above	beside	into	throughout
across	besides	like	till
after	between	near	to
against	beyond	of	toward
along	but	off	under
alongside	by	on	underneath
among	despite	onto	until
around	down	out	up
as	during	outside	upon
at	except	over	with
before	for	past	within
behind	from	round	without

MORE

SEE ALSO
Subordinating
Conjunctions,
p. 79

Some of the words on this list are not always prepositions. For example, **about, since,** and **until** can also be conjunctions. It depends on how the word is used in a particular sentence.

Compound Prepositions

Compound prepositions are two or more words working together like a one-word preposition. Here are some examples:

according to	in back of
ahead of	in case of
along with	in front of
as for	in regard to
away from	in spite of
because of	instead of
by way of	out of
due to	up to
except for	with the exception of
in addition to	

Every teacher **with the exception of** Ms. Blumenthal is out sick.

Every teacher **except** Ms. Blumenthal is out sick.

Prepositional Phrases

A **prepositional phrase** is a group of two or more words that begins with a preposition and ends with a noun or pronoun called the **object of the preposition.** Every preposition has an object.

SEE ALSO
**Eight Uses of Nouns:
Object of a Preposition,
pp. 38-39
Personal Pronouns:
Object of a Preposition,
p. 44**

Sometimes the object of the preposition is the very next word after the preposition:

Preposition	Object of the Preposition
near	me
at	school
with	Eddie

Or, it can come a few words later.

Preposition		Object of the Preposition
in spite of	the terrible	weather
inside	the man's jacket	pocket
throughout	his long and illustrious	career

A **prepositional phrase** includes the preposition, the object of the preposition, and all words in between.

You can have as many prepositional phrases in a sentence as you need. For example, here's the first line of a well-known song.

Over the river and through the woods to Grandmother's house we go.

Conjunctions

What is a conjunction?

A **conjunction** is a word that joins other words or parts of sentences together. Conjunctions are like glue.

▶ Here are examples of conjunctions joining words together:

David **and** Jennifer are brother **and** sister.

The weather forecaster predicted snow **or** sleet today.

▶ Here are examples of conjunctions joining parts of a sentence together:

I ran as fast as I could; **however,** I still missed the pie-throwing contest.

I'll call the Department of Sanitation **if** you don't get that filthy animal out of here.

Kinds of Conjunctions

▶ **Coordinating Conjunctions**

Coordinating conjunctions join words, phrases, and sentences (independent clauses) together.

and	nor	but	for	yet	so	or

2▶ Subordinating Conjunctions

A **subordinating conjunction** joins a dependent clause to an independent clause.

after	before	so	till	where
although	for	so that	unless	whereas
as	if	than	until	wherever
as if	once	that	when	whether
because	since	though	whenever	while

While you mind the baby, I'm going shopping.

I'm never talking to him again **unless** he tells me the secret.

A few of these same words can be used as prepositions in other sentences.

since yesterday   **after** the swim meet   **until** graduation

for her sake   **before** the judge   **till** tomorrow

SEE ALSO
Master List of
One-Word
Prepositions,
p. 75

3▶ Correlative Conjunctions

Correlative conjunctions are used in pairs, but the pair is split up by other words.

both/and	either/or	neither/nor
whether/or	just as/so	not only/but also

MORE ▶

Both the giraffe **and** the chimpanzee have the hiccups.

Either you give me that letter **or** I'll tell the mailman.

Neither the mother **nor** the father knows about the cat.

▶ Adverbial Conjunctions (Conjunctive Adverbs)

Adverbial conjunctions join clauses of equal value. They are like coordinating conjunctions because they join independent clauses together to make compound sentences.

accordingly	consequently	moreover
hence	however	nevertheless	therefore

To learn how to punctuate sentences with adverbial conjunctions, see page 95.

Master List of Conjunctions

after	but	not only/but also	unless
although	either/or	once	until
and	even though	or	when
as	for	since	whenever
as if	however	so	where
as soon as	if	so that	whereas
as though	in order that	than	wherever
because	just as/so	that	whether
before	neither/nor	though	while
both/and	nor	till	yet

Interjections

What is an interjection?

Interjections are special words that show strong feelings or emotions like excitement, happiness, horror, shock, sadness, pain, anger, and disgust. Interjections usually come at the beginning of a sentence. You use them to add punch or energy to stories. Don't use them too much. When you overdo interjections, they lose their power.

Sometimes interjections are just sounds, shouts, gasps, or exclamations, more like noises than regular words.

Here are some common interjections:				
Aha	Gosh	Whoopee	Super	Yoo-hoo
Ahem	Hello	Oh	Ugh	Gee Whiz
All right	Help	Oh, no	Well	Good grief
Dear me	Hey	Ooops	Nuts	Right on
Gadzooks	Hooray	Ouch	Wow	Yippee
My Goodness	Indeed	Phew	Yikes	Yuck

By the way, you can make up your own energetic interjections like

Horsefeathers! She fell off the bronco.

Yazoo! The tornado is over.

Greasy grasshoppers! This street is slippery.

IVAN CAPP

The eight parts of speech are the building blocks of any language.

Whenever you speak, whenever you read something or write something, whenever you use words, you are using the parts of speech.

To help remember them, think of **IVAN CAPP**. Each of the letters in his name is the first letter of one of the parts of speech.

I   - interjection

V   - verb

A   - adjective

N   - noun

C   - conjunction

A   - adverb

P   - pronoun

P   - preposition

Style & Usage

Punctuation Rules Everybody Needs

When and Why to CAPITALIZE a Word

Good Spelling Rules to Use Every Day

Preventing Double Negatives

Avoiding Sexist Language

Homonyms: Words That Sound Alike but Are Spelled Differently

100 Easily Confused and Misused Words

Contractions: Shrinking Words

Building Compound Words

Idioms: When Words Mean More Than They Say

Initials, Acronyms, and Abbreviations

Punctuation Rules Everybody Needs

Apostrophes

SEE ALSO
Contractions:
Shrinking
Words,
pp. 126-128
Possessive
Nouns,
pp. 39-40

Use apostrophes:

▶ in contractions

I'm sorry that she's coming after you've left.

▶ in possessive nouns

Sybil's cousin found Doug's umbrellas in the Goldins' car.

▶ when you refer to the plural of letters and words

*There are four **s**'s, four **i**'s, and two **p**'s in Mississippi.*

*You have too many **very**'s in your essay.*

Colons

Use colons:

▶ after the greeting in a business letter

Dear Sirs: Dear Ms. Freedman: Dear Chairperson:

▶ to introduce a list

You will need the following clothes for the camping trip: boots, gloves, a heavy jacket, scarf, and a hat.

▶ between the hour and the minutes when you use numbers to express time

> 4:34 p.m.   12:52 a.m.

▶ to introduce a long direct quotation

At the press conference, the President declared:

> Times are getting better. The economy is starting to improve, more people are working, crime is down, reading scores are up, the air is getting cleaner, people are buying more homes, factories are humming, and my pet cat just had six adorable kittens.

Notice that you don't use quotation marks with a long direct quotation. Instead, you indent on both sides from the main text.

Commas

Put a comma:

▶ before a conjunction that joins the independent clauses in a compound sentence

> My uncle loves to dance, and my aunt plays the piano.

SEE ALSO
Compound Sentences, pp. 16-17
Complex Sentences, p. 17

▶ after a dependent clause that comes at the beginning of a complex sentence

> Even though I forgot to study, I still did well on the test.

▶ between a city and a state
    Boston, Massachusetts

▶ between the day and year in a date
    August 14, 1941

(Don't put a comma in a date if it's only the month and the year —August 1941)

▶ to separate three or more words or phrases in a series
    For my birthday I want a video game, an underwater watch, and a butterfly net.

▶ after the greeting and closing in a friendly letter
    Dear Ms. Youngman,   Sincerely yours,

▶ after introductory words at the beginnings of sentences
    No, you can't dye your hair green.

▶ after mild interjections
    Oh, I didn't know today was the big day.

▶ to set off the person you're speaking to
    Lenny, I've been expecting you since Friday.
    I've been expecting you, my tardy friend, since Friday.

▶ to set off appositives
    Jen, the craziest kid in our class, scored the most points.

▶ with words that interrupt the basic idea of the sentence

Aunt Roslyn, of course, would not wear the parrot costume.
George, therefore, had to leave the drugstore in a hurry.

▶ to separate two adjectives that modify the same noun

The huge, furry dog chased him over the fence and into the pool.

If you're not sure whether or not to put a comma between two adjectives in a row, ask yourself if you can substitute "and" for the comma. "The huge (and) furry dog" gets a comma but not "the spoiled (and) turkey sandwich."

T
I
P

▶ in front of short direct quotations in the middle of a sentence

Then he asked, "How did you get here without a balloon?"

▶ at the end of a direct quotation that is a statement (not a question or an exclamation) when it comes at the beginning of a sentence

"Today must be Tuesday," she muttered.

Dashes

Use dashes:

▶ before and after comments, questions, exclamations, or other interrupters that you write into a sentence to give information or add extra emphasis

Two rooms — the cafeteria and the library — were flooded. The mayor — he's my aunt's boyfriend — came to the assembly today.

▶ to introduce a list of items

The teacher said that these were the five most important steps in doing our homework — write it down, take it home, do it, bring it back, hand it in.

> **T**
> **I**
> **P**
>
> You can use dashes instead of other punctuation marks like parentheses, commas, or colons to show more emphasis, add information, or create special effects. Don't overdo any one kind of punctuation mark. Use variety in your writing.

▶ after an interrupted or unfinished statement or thought

I knew it couldn't possibly be Nita, and yet —

Ellipses

Ellipses are three or four dots in a row. Ellipses replace words that have been left out. Use three dots to show that words have been left out in the middle of a passage:

> I pledge allegiance to the flag of the United States of America and to the republic for which it stands. One nation... with Liberty and Justice for all.

Use four dots if the words left out come at the end of the sentence:

> To be or not to be ....
> William Shakespeare

Exclamation Points

Put an exclamation point:

SEE ALSO Interjections, p. 81

▶ after strong interjections

> Oh, no! I lost my mother's earrings!

after exclamatory sentences

I can't stand this place anymore!

SEE ALSO
Exclamatory
Sentences,
p. 15
Imperative
Sentences,
pp. 14-15

after strong imperative sentences

Sit down and be quiet, you nut!

Hyphens

Use a hyphen:

to break a word between syllables at end of a line

The famous Italian sculptor, painter, and archi-tect, Michelangelo, was born in 1475.

in two-part numbers from twenty-one to ninety-nine written as words

twenty-one   fifty-three   sixty-eight

in fractions written as words

one-third   two-fifths   fifteen-sixteenths

SEE ALSO
Building
Compound
Words,
pp. 129-130

in some compound nouns and adjectives

well-known   know-it-all   drive-in

Parentheses

Use parentheses:

▶ to give the reader extra information

To order the Gut Buster, call our toll-free number (800-GUT-BUST).

For more on short giraffes, read chapter 12 (pages 27-38).

▶ around the abbreviation or acronym of an organization or company after you've written its full name

She worked for the National Aeronautics and Space Administration (NASA).

▶ to put a statement, question, direction, or exclamation, or some other information that's not really part of the sentence into the sentence. (You do this for extra effect, as in this case.)

She got help from Dave (He's a brain) and still flunked the test.

You can use a question mark or an exclamation point — but not a period — at the end of an expression in parentheses when it's in the middle of a sentence.

Jen's cousin Cindy (Do you know her?) moved back to Chicago.

T
I
P

Periods

SEE ALSO
Declarative
Sentences
p. 14
Imperative
Sentences,
pp. 14-15

Put a period:

▶ at the end of a declarative sentence

The batteries in my cassette player are dead.

▶ at the end of an imperative sentence that makes a request, gives an instruction, or states a mild order

Always shut off the computer when you're finished.

▶ after most initials

John F. Kennedy

SEE ALSO
How to Use
Abbreviations,
p. 138

▶ after most abbreviations

P.O. Box 325

116 Binghamton Ave.

Mt. Renae, CA

 EXCEPTION Do not use a period with the postal service abbreviation of a state. Examples: MA, NY, FL

Question Marks

SEE ALSO
Interrogative
Sentences,
p. 14

Put a question mark:

▶ At the end of a question

Why are you doing that disgusting thing?

Don't use a question mark after a polite request that sounds like a question but really isn't:

Will you please sign your name here.

Quotation Marks

Always put quotation marks before and after the names of:

▶ articles in magazines and newspapers

I cut out " The Amazing Life of a Hummingbird " from Sunday's paper.

▶ chapters in books

Read the chapter called "The Boy from the Clouds" for homework.

▶ essays and short stories

My sister's essay, "How to Improve This School," won the award!

The story "Dark and Stormy Night" was scary, but funny.

▶ songs and poems

For the talent show I'm singing "Dragon, Why Are You Dragging?"

"Love Among Petunias" is in the literary magazine.

Use quotation marks:

▶ to set off words or phrases that are special for any reason

> I got "ambidextrous" right on the spelling test.
>
> He explained "the pursuit of happiness" in class yesterday.

▶ before and after a direct quotation (someone's exact words)

T I P

Notice that periods, commas, and other punctuation marks that end or interrupt a quotation go inside the second set of quotation marks.

> Mary said, "I haven't seen such a mess since the last tornado."
>
> "I haven't seen such a mess since the last tornado," said Mary.
>
> "I haven't seen such a mess," said Mary, "since the last tornado."
>
> "I haven't seen such a mess in ages," said Mary. "The last time was the last tornado."

Do not use quotation marks with an **indirect quotation**, words that do not quote someone exactly:

> Mary said that she hadn't seen such a mess since the last tornado.

Single Quotation Marks

Use only one quotation mark at either end when a quote is written within another quote:

> "Ellen, I still haven't seen your report on 'Malcolm X: By Any Means Necessary'," said Ms. Baldwin.

Semicolons

Use a semicolon:

▶

to join the independent clauses of a compound sentence together when you don't use a comma and a conjunction

Chorus meets every Tuesday; band rehearsal is on Wednesday.

▶

in front of some conjunctions that join together two simple sentences into one compound sentence. In these cases, put a semicolon in front of the conjunction and a comma after it.

I usually like pecan pie; however, today I don't want any.

She's been absent this week; therefore, she hasn't read the book.

You've been mean to me all day; nevertheless, I'll still help you.

SEE ALSO
Compound
Sentences,
pp. 16-17

SEE ALSO
Adverbial
Conjunctions,
p. 80

MORE ➡

Other conjunctions and phrases punctuated this way:	
accordingly	in addition
also	indeed
as a result	in fact
besides	moreover
consequently	on the contrary
for example	on the other hand
for instance	otherwise
for this reason	that is
furthermore	thus
hence	yet

▶ in a series of three or more items when commas are used within the items

> Appearing on tonight's show are Brenda, the wonder frog; Tulip, the talking toucan; and Henrietta, the hip hippo.

Underlining

In handwritten or typed work, underline the names of:

▶ books, magazines, and newspapers

> Did you read <u>My Teacher Is from Mars</u>?
>
> I have a subscription to <u>Bullfrogs and Toads</u> magazine.
>
> Her picture is in the <u>Daily Herald-Gazette</u> today.

▶ movies, plays, musicals, operas, and television shows

> I never go to horror movies like <u>Flying Snakes Eat Cleveland.</u>

> Last night we saw <u>Tosca</u> at the opera house.

> For graduation my class is putting on <u>Abe Lincoln in the White House.</u>

> <u>Fearless Fred</u>, my favorite show, is on Channel 6 tonight!

In books or other printed works, the names of books, movies, magazines, etc., are often printed in **italics** instead of being underlined. When words are italicized, the letters slant.

> There's a review of *The Secrets of the Aardvark* in today's *Tribune*.

When and Why to CAPITALIZE a Word

To **capitalize** means to begin a word with a capital letter.

You should always capitalize:

▶ the first word in a sentence

When it rains, the cat stays indoors.

▶ the pronoun **I**

At the game, I shouted my voice out.

▶ proper nouns

Jessica, Empire State Building, Chicago

▶ proper adjectives

French, American, Californian, Dutch, Israeli

SEE ALSO Proper Nouns, pp. 31-32 Proper Adjectives p. 66

▶ titles that show the rank or position of people when used with their names

Captain Kilmer   Dr. Smith   Mrs. Levine

Chief Gerson   King Charles   President Lincoln

▶ a person's title when it is used in place of the person's name

Congratulations, General. The war is over.

Do not capitalize a title used without a person's name unless you're addressing the person directly.

King, did you know that the queen asked the prime minister to call a doctor?

NOT *The Queen asked the Prime Minister...*

▶ family members

You capitalize family members when the words stand alone in a sentence without a possessive pronoun or when they are followed by a person's name.

I told Uncle George to meet Grandpa at the drugstore.

▶ days of the week and months of the year

Sunday, Monday, Tuesday, Wednesday, Thursday, Friday, Saturday

January, February, March, April, May, June, July, August, September, October, November, December

Do not capitalize the four seasons of the year.

spring, summer, winter, fall (or autumn)

▶ the first word in the greeting of a friendly letter

Dear Henny,   Dear friends,   My dear students,   **MORE**

▶ the first word in the closing of a letter

    Very truly yours,   *Best wishes,*   *Warmest regards,*

▶ all the words in the greeting of a business letter

    My Dear Madam: *Dear Fellow Students:*

▶ the first, last, and all the main words in the title of a:

    book: *The Last of the Mohicans*

    movie: *The Wizard of Oz*

    song: *The Star Spangled Banner*

    play or musical: *Phantom of the Opera*

    magazine: *National Geographic*

    newspaper: *The New York Times*

    television show: *Charles in Charge*

"Main words" generally means everything except short prepositions, conjunctions, or articles (**the, an,** and **a**).

▶ school subjects when they are the names of languages or specific courses listed in the school catalogue.

    Spanish   *Honors Biology*   *Science 3*

(but NOT just plain mathematics, science, or history)

▶ geographic locations when they refer to specific areas on the map

North, South, East, West, the Middle East, the Far East

(but NOT just directions)

Geographical location: I lived in the West for four years.
Direction: He headed west, Sheriff.

▶ national and local holidays

Thanksgiving	Veterans Day	Labor Day
Memorial Day	Martin Luther King, Jr.'s Birthday	
Brooklyn Week	Firefighters Day	Fourth of July
	Turnip Festival	

▶ religious holidays

Good Friday   Passover   Idul-Fitr

Good Spelling Rules to Use Every Day

Spelling words in English can be tricky. When you're in doubt, it's a good idea to check your dictionary. These nine rules can guide you, but be sure to check the exceptions.

1 - 5. Adding suffixes (or endings)

▶ When you add **full** to any word, drop the second l.

awe + full = awful

beauty + full = beautiful

cheer + full = cheerful

cup + full = cupful

faith + full = faithful

forget + full = forgetful

grace + full = graceful

harm + full = harmful

mouth + full = mouthful

pain + full = painful

peace + full = peaceful

play + full = playful

power + full = powerful

spoon + full = spoonful

thank + full = thankful

thought + full = thoughtful

(You sometimes have to make other small changes, too. For example: beauty + full = beautiful.)

▶ When you add a **y** or a suffix that begins with a vowel **(a, e, i, o, u)**, to a word that ends with a silent **e**, drop the silent **e**.

Word ends with silent e		Suffix begins with a vowel or is **y**		Drop the e
abuse	+	ive	=	abusive
convene	+	ient	=	convenient
divide	+	ing	=	dividing
dose	+	age	=	dosage
endure	+	ance	=	endurance
fortune	+	ate	=	fortunate
joke	+	ed	=	joked
love	+	able	=	lovable
nature	+	al	=	natural
pure	+	er	=	purer
reverse	+	ible	=	reversible
scare	+	y	=	scary
tame	+	est	=	tamest

When you add a suffix that begins with a vowel to most words that end with the letters **ge** or **ce**, do not drop the final **e**:

change	+	able	=	changeable
notice	+	able	=	noticeable

Adding the suffix **age** to some words:

acre	+	age	=	acreage
mile	+	age	=	mileage

EXCEPTION

3▶ When adding the suffix **ing** to a word that ends with **ie**, drop the **e** and change the **i** to **y**.

Word ends with ie				Change to y
die	+	ing	=	dying
lie	+	ing	=	lying
tie	+	ing	=	tying

EXCEPTION

dye	+	ing	=	dyeing (my hair)
canoe	+	ing	=	canoeing (down the river)
hoe	+	ing	=	hoeing (the field)
shoe	+	ing	=	shoeing (a horse)
singe	+	ing	=	singeing (the dress while ironing carelessly)

4▶ When adding a suffix that begins with a consonant (all letters that aren't vowels or **y**), do not drop the silent **e**.

Word ends with with silent e		Suffix begins with a consonant		Don't drop the e
arrange	+	ment	=	arrangement
care	+	less	=	careless
forgive	+	ness	=	forgiveness
safe	+	ty	=	safety
sincere	+	ly	=	sincerely

Drop the silent **e** when adding a suffix beginning with a consonant to the following words:

acknowledge	+	ment	=	acknowledgment
argue	+	ment	=	argument
awe	+	full	=	awful
horrible	+	ly	=	horribly
incredible	+	ly	=	incredibly
judge	+	ment	=	judgment
nine	+	th	=	ninth
possible	+	ly	=	possibly
terrible	+	ly	=	terribly
true	+	ly	=	truly
twelve	+	th	=	twelfth
wise	+	dom	=	wisdom
whole	+	ly	=	wholly
wide	+	th	=	width

5▶ Double the final consonant when you're adding a suffix that begins with a vowel (**ing, ed**) to a word that ends with a vowel and a consonant (**hop, refer**).

MORE ▶

One -syllable word ends with single vowel + single consonant		Suffix begins with a vowel		Double the final consonant
bag	+	age	=	baggage
begin	+	ing	=	beginning
big	+	est	=	biggest
control	+	able	=	controllable
forbid	+	en	=	forbidden
get	+	ing	=	getting
quit	+	er	=	quitter
rebel	+	ion	=	rebellion
regret	+	able	=	regrettable
skip	+	ed	=	skipped
submit	+	ed	=	submitted
transmit	+	er	=	transmitter

EXCEPTION

If the accent does not fall on the last syllable, do not double the final consonant:

BEN-efit	+	ed	=	benefited
CAN-cel	+	ed	=	canceled
COL-or	+	ing	=	coloring
EN-ter	+	ing	=	entering
LA-bel	+	ed	=	labeled
PI-lot	+	ed	=	piloted
SHOV-el	+	ing	=	shoveling

6 - 8. Making nouns plural

To make most nouns plural, you just add **s**. However, there are exceptions. For example:

6▶ Add **s** to make a word plural if it ends
with **y** and the letter in front of the **y**
is a vowel **(a, e, i, o, u)**.

    1 ray   —   2 rays
    1 turkey —   2 turkeys

7▶ Drop the **y** and add **ies**
if the letter in front of the
final **y** is a consonant.

    1 country —   2 countries
    1 puppy   —   2 puppies

Just add s (The letter before the y is a vowel)		Drop the final y and add ies (The letter before the y is a consonant)	
attorney	+ s	baby	babies
birthday	+ s	country	countries
boy	+ s	cry	cries
chimney	+ s	diary	diaries
essay	+ s	dictionary	dictionaries
highway	+ s	fry	fries
journey	+ s	jury	juries
joy	+ s	laboratory	laboratories
phoney	+ s	lady	ladies
play	+ s	library	libraries
stay	+ s	sky	skies
valley	+ s	story	stories
way	+ s	try	tries

8 Add **s** to most nouns that end in **o** to make them plural:

banjos	patios	pimentos	solos
cellos	photos	radios	sopranos
duos	pianos	rodeos	stereos
lassos	piccolos	shampoos	trios

A few exceptions add **es**:

Singular	Plural
echo	echoes
embargo	embargoes
hero	heroes
potato	potatoes
tomato	tomatoes
torpedo	torpedoes
veto	vetoes

Bonus Some **o** nouns can be made plural by adding either **s** or **es**.

Singular	Plural
domino	dominos or dominoes
halo	halos or haloes
mosquito	mosquitos or mosquitoes
motto	mottos or mottoes
volcano	volcanos or volcanoes
zero	zeros or zeroes

9. Using i and e

....

i before e

except after **c**

or when sounding like **a**

as in **neighbor** and **weigh**

There are many words that follow this rhyming rule perfectly. Here are some of them:

i before e	except after c	or when sounding like a as in neighbor and weigh
achievement	ceiling	beige
believe	conceit	eighty
brief	conceited	freight
chief	conceive	neigh
die	deceit	reign
grief	deceive	sleigh
lie	perceive	vein
pie	receive	veil
retrieve	receipt	weight
tie		reindeer
unwieldy		

Here are many of the words that break the rule:

ancient	forfeit	scientist
being	heifer	seismologist
counterfeit	height	seize
efficient	heir	sheik
(also deficient,	kaleidoscope	sleight
proficient, and	leisure	society
sufficient)	neither	species
either	protein	stein
financier	(also caffeine	their
foreign	and codeine)	weird

EXCEPTION

An Exceptional Sentence

If you learn this sentence, you will know many of the rule-breaker words. If the word is in the sentence, it breaks the rule in the "i before e" poem.

Rule-Breaker Sentence

Neither a financier seizing counterfeit money, nor
a weird sovereign from a foreign society, nor
a sleight seismologist with a species of heifer, nor
a leisurely sheik with an ancient kaleidoscope, nor
an heir of great height with a conscience, nor
an efficient scientist with protein forfeited their steins.

Preventing Double Negatives

Negative Words

Negative means **no**. A negative word expresses a meaning that is the opposite of positive. It says that something is not, rather than that something is.

Negative word	Positive Opposite
no	yes, any
nobody	somebody, anybody
nothing	something, anything
nowhere	somewhere, anywhere
none	some, any
never	sometimes, often, ever
no one	someone, anyone
nor	or
neither	either
not	is

Although most negative words begin with an **n, hardly, scarcely,** and **barely** are also negative.

Negative Contractions

Not is one of the most frequently used negative words. The contraction for **not** is **n't**, so any contraction that ends in **n't** is a negative word.

aren't	can't	couldn't	didn't
doesn't	don't	hasn't	hadn't
haven't	isn't	mustn't	shouldn't
wasn't	weren't	wouldn't	won't (positive: will)

Ways to Prevent Double Negatives

Use only one negative word in a sentence to convey a negative meaning. If you say

> *Nobody wants none of your pie.*

you are really saying that everybody wants some of the pie. Two negatives make a positive.

Two Ways to Correct a Double Negative

▶ 1. Change a negative word into a positive word. If there is a negative contraction, you can either take it out of the sentence or drop the **n't** at the end.

Double negative: *They don't have nothing to wear to the party.*
Correct sentences: *They don't have anything to wear to the party.*
They have nothing to wear to the party.

Double negative: *She can't tell nobody about this.*
Correct sentences: *She can't tell anybody about this.*
She can tell nobody about this.

▶ 2. To correct double negatives that contain **hardly, barely,** or **scarcely**, change the other negative word into a positive word.

Double negative: *She had hardly nothing left of her sandwich.*
Correct sentence: *She had hardly anything left of her sandwich.*

Avoiding Sexist Language

In the past, the noun **man** referred to all human beings regardless of whether they were men or women. **Mankind** was used to mean humankind. In the same way, the masculine pronouns **he, his, him,** and **himself** referred not only to boys and men, but also to girls and women.

> *Tell a person who wants to succeed that he should work hard.*
>
> *Everyone should take out his spelling book.*
>
> *Throughout history, man has struggled to keep himself free.*

Today, many writers and speakers try to avoid sentences like those. After all, shouldn't girls work hard too? Unless it's an all-boys school, shouldn't the girls take out their spelling books? And since the beginning of time, haven't girls and women fought for freedom too?

Ways to Avoid Sexist Language

▶ Find new ways to include feminine pronouns (**she, her, herself**) along with the masculine pronouns:

> *Tell a person who wants to succeed that **he or she** must work hard.*
>
> *Everyone should take out **his or her** spelling book.*

But it can get awkward and wordy if you always try to include both sexes equally in everything you write.

> *If a student wants to audition for the play, he or she should bring his or her script to the auditorium after his or her last class today.*

SEE ALSO
Collective
Nouns,
p. 33
Five Other
Kinds of
Pronouns,
pp. 49-51

▶ A way of solving this kind of **he/she, him/her, his/her** problem is to use neutral nouns and pronouns or to use plural nouns and pronouns instead of singular ones:

> *Anyone who wants to succeed should work hard.*
>
> *Class, take out your spelling books.*
>
> *Throughout history, people have struggled to keep themselves free.*
>
> *Students auditioning for the play should bring their scripts to the auditorium after their last classes today.*

▶ Some people are using a newly created pronoun, **s/he,** to stand for **she** and **he.**

> *If a person wishes to enter the contest, **s/he** should submit an entry form immediately.*

But it's not clear yet if enough people will use **s/he** for it to become an accepted and natural part of our language.

▶ Many people prefer to drop the feminine noun altogether or use a new form. For example, **actress, fireman,** and **mailman** become **actor, fire fighter,** and **mail carrier.**

Homonyms:

Words That Sound Alike but Are Spelled Differently

Homonyms, or homophones, are words that are spelled differently, have different meanings, but are pronounced alike. Usually they come in pairs. Sometimes they come in triplets. Here are some of the most common.

allowed, *adj.* permitted
aloud, *adv.* out loud; with noise
Strict librarian: *You are not **allowed** to talk **aloud** here.*

ant, *n.* tiny insect
aunt, *n.* your parent's sister or your uncle's wife
Uncle: *Look at the little **ant** climbing on the shoe of your **aunt**.*

ate, *v.* past tense of "to eat"
eight, *n.* the number between seven and nine
Jet traveler: *Yesterday I **ate** breakfast at **eight** p.m.!*

bear, *n.* a big, furry animal
bare, *adj.* naked
Shocked zookeeper: *Bear, you're **bare**! Put your fur on.*

blue, *n.* a color
blew, *v.* past tense of "to blow"
Modern nursery rhyme: *Little Boy **Blue** really **blew** his horn.*

break, *v.* to make come apart
brake, *n.* a device for stopping a vehicle
Driving teacher: *Don't press too hard or you'll **break** the **brake**.*

bury, *v.* to put something into the earth
berry, *n.* a small, pulpy fruit with seeds
Detective: *Why would the dog **bury** the **berry** in the garden?*

capital, *adj.* main, principal, chief
capitol, *n.* the building in which the legislature meets
Tour guide: *In the **capital** city, you'll visit the **capitol** building.*

n.	=	noun
v.	=	verb
adj.	=	adjective
adv.	=	adverb
conj.	=	conjunction
pron.	=	pronoun

close, *v.* to shut; to block an entrance or opening
clothes, *n.* articles of clothing
Mother: Close the door to the **clothes** closet.

dear, *n.* greatly loved person
deer, *n.* forest animal like a moose or elk
Girlfriend: Dear, look at that darling **deer.**

fair, *adj.* just; impartial; according to accepted rules
fare, *n.* the cost of a ride on a train, bus, plane, etc.
Annoyed bus rider: I don't think it's **fair** to charge an extra **fare.**

feat, *n.* an act or deed that shows great strength, courage, or skill
feet, *n.* plural of "foot"
Marathon winner: I owe this great **feat** to my great **feet.**

flew, *v.* past tense of "to fly"
flu, *n.* short for "influenza," a highly contagious disease
Sick pilot: I **flew** the plane even though I had the **flu.**

flour, *n.* fine, ground grain used for baking
flower, *n.* the blossom or bloom on a plant
Fancy baker: This **flour** is made of **flower** petals.

heard, *v.* past tense of the verb "to hear"
herd, *n.* a group of large animals like cattle or sheep
Angry cowboy: I **heard** what you said about my **herd!**

he'll, contraction for "he will"
heal, *v.* to make well; cure
heel, *n.* the rounded, rear part of the human foot, below the ankle
Foot doctor's nurse: He'll try to **heal** your sore **heel.**

here, *adv.* at or in this place
hear, *v.* to receive sounds in the ear
Telephone repairer: Here, see if you can **hear** with this phone.

lone, *adj.* alone
loan, *n.* a sum of money lent at interest
Banker: Do you think you're the **lone** person who needs a **loan?**

mail, *n.* letters or packages sent through the post office
male, *n.* a man
Post office rule: A **mail** carrier can be **male** or female.

Maine, *n.* a state in New England.
main, *adj.* the greatest in size or importance; chief; principal
mane, *n.* long, heavy hair around the neck of some animals
New England stable owner: In **Maine,** the **main** thing is to brush the horse's **mane** regularly.

meet, *v.* to make the acquaintance of someone
meat, *n.* flesh of animals used as food
Strict vegetarian: I don't want to **meet** someone who eats **meat**.

no, *adv.* certainly not; not so
know, *v.* to be certain of the facts; to understand clearly
Student who didn't study: **No**, I don't **know** the answer.

our, *pron.* belongs to us
hour, *n.* sixty minutes
Noisy kids: **Our** mother told us to be quiet for an **hour**.

pain, *n.* a feeling of hurt, suffering, or physical distress
pane, *n.* a sheet of glass placed in a window
Angry house owner: What a **pain**! My window **pane** is broken.

pale, *adj.* without healthy color
pail, *n.* a round, open container for carrying water, sand, etc.
Storyteller: Jack and Jill turned **pale** when they lost their **pail**.

pear, *n.* a fruit shaped like a bell
pair, *n.* a set of two things
Math teacher: One **pear** and one **pear** equal a **pair** of **pears**.

piece, *n.* a part of something
peace, *n.* freedom from war or fighting; calmness
History museum guide: This **piece** of paper is the **peace** treaty.

plane, *n.* an airplane
plain, *n.* an area of flat land; or *adj.* ordinary
Bored pilot: We're landing the **plane** on the **plain**, flat **plain** again .

pray, *v.* to ask or beg for something
prey, *v.* to hunt a living thing
Man lost in woods: I **pray** that an animal doesn't **prey** on me.

principal, *n.* the head of a school
principle, *n.* a rule of personal behavior
Proud pupil: Our **principal** is a person of very high **principle**.

reign, *n.* the period that a monarch (king or queen) rules
rein, *n.* straps attached to the sides of a horse's mouth for riding
rain, *n.* drops of water that fall from the sky
Royal historian: During her **reign**, the queen always held the **rein** during a heavy **rain**.

roll, *n.* a list of names
role, *n.* a part in a play or movie
Movie director: Call the **roll** of people who want to play this **role**.

sail, *n.* canvas that catches the wind and causes a boat to move
sale, *n.* the selling of goods for less than the usual cost
Budget-minded boat owner: I'll get a new **sail** when they're on **sale**.

seen, *v.* past participle of "to see"
scene, *n.* an episode, especially in a play, movie, or television show
One movie fan to another: *You should have seen that scene!*

sent, *v.* past tense of "to send"
cent, *n.* a penny
scent, *n.* an odor, smell, or aroma
Girl: *I sent my boyfriend with a cent to buy me a pretty scent.*

soar, *v.* to fly upward
sore, *adj.* painful
Baby bird: *After I soar over the mountains, my wings are sore.*

some, *adj.* a portion; a few, or remarkable; striking
sum, *n.* an amount of money
Student looking at a long addition problem: *Some kids would say that's some big sum!*

son, *n.* male child
sun, *n.* the hot, bright star that is the center of our solar system
Father: *Son, our closest star is the sun.*

stare, *v.* to look at for a long time
stair, *n.* a step
Gentleman: *I can't help but stare at the lovely lady on the stair.*

stationary, *adj.* not moving
stationery, *n.* writing paper, envelopes, etc.
Mother to restless child: *Stay stationary in the stationery store.*

steal, *v.* to take something without permission
steel, *n.* an alloy of iron mixed with carbon
Judge to thief: *You are guilty of trying to steal the steel.*

tale, *n.* a story
tail, *n.* part of an animal's body that sticks out from its main part
Jungle guide: *I'll tell you an amazing tale about a tiger's tail.*

there, *adv.* at or in that place
their, *pron.* belonging to them
they're, contraction for "they are"
Eyewitness to police: *They're over there in their secret hideout.*

threw, *v.* past tense of "to throw"
through, *prep.* in one side of something and out the other
Sportscaster: *He threw the ball through the scoreboard!*

to, *prep.* toward
two, *n.* and *adj.* the number between one and three
too, *adv.* also; in addition; also, more than enough
One movie fan to another: *I went to the movies and saw two films, too.*

wait, *v.* to stop or stay in place, expecting something to happen
weight, *n.* the heaviness of something
Trainer to athlete: *Wait a minute. I need to know your weight.*

waste, *v.* to make poor use of something
waist, *n.* part of the body around the middle
Dieter: *I hate to waste food, but it will all end up on my waist.*

way, *n.* the form or method of doing something
weigh, *v.* to find out how heavy something is
Scale demonstrator: *This is the way you weigh yourself.*

week, *n.* seven days
weak, *adj.* not strong
Overworked student: *At the end of each week I feel weak.*

where, *adv.* in what place
wear, *v.* to have clothes on the body
Shopper: *Where would I ever wear a dress like that?*

whether, *conj.* if; either
weather, *n.* the condition of the atmosphere
Meteorologist: *I don't know whether tomorrow's weather will be good or bad.*

which, *pron.* a word that asks questions about people and things
witch, *n.* a woman with evil supernatural powers
Halloween judge: *Which of the witch costumes is ugliest?*

whole, *adj.* complete; entire
hole, *n.* an opening in the ground
Boss to ditchdigger: *Dig this hole for the whole day.*

won, *v.* past tense of "to win"
one, *n.* and *adj.* the first and lowest whole number
Sportscaster: *The team won only one game the whole season.*

write, *v.* to make letters and words with a pen or pencil
right, *adj.* the opposite of left; also, correct
Penmanship teacher: *Write with your left or right hand. They're both right.*

AUNT

ANT

100 Easily Confused and Misused Words

In English some words sound and look very much like other words. They can be easily confused and misused. Here are 100 of the trickiest of these words.

n. = **noun**	**v.** = **verb**	**adj.** = **adjective**
adv. = **adverb**	**pron.** = **pronoun**	

accent, *n.* a manner of speech characteristic of a certain city, country, or region
ascent, *n.* the act of going up
*In a French **accent** he told about his **ascent** of the mountain.*

accept, *v.* to take what is offered or given
except, *prep.* leaving out; other than
*They will **accept** everyone into the club **except** him.*

adapt, *v.* to change or adjust to a different situation
adept, *adj.* very skilled; expert in something
adopt, *v.* to choose an idea to follow as one's own
*He's not **adept** when he has to **adopt** new ideas or **adapt** to new situations.*

affect, *v.* to influence, to change
effect, *n.* a result, a consequence
*The student government hopes this meeting will **affect** (change) school rules. We think our suggestions will have a good **effect** (result) on student life.*

alley, *n.* a narrow street or passageway
ally, *n.* a person or country united with another for a common purpose
*Follow him quickly! He ducked down the **alley** with his closest **ally**.*

all ready, everyone or everything is prepared
already, *adv.* previously; before this time; by this time
*We were **all ready** for the class trip, but the bus had **already** left.*

allusion, *n.* a mention or suggestion made indirectly or in passing
illusion, *n.* a false or misleading idea or belief; an unreal image
*Are you making an **allusion** to the Wizard of Oz with your red shoes, or is it just an **illusion**?*

altogether, *adv.* completely; in all
all together, at the same time; in the same place
*The conductor was **altogether** disgusted when the orchestra couldn't play the notes **all together**.*

anecdote, *n.* a short account of an incident or event
antidote, *n.* a remedy that counteracts the effects of poison
*She told me an **anecdote** about the time she used her grandmother's **antidote** when she was bitten by a poisonous snake.*

angel, *n.* an immortal, spiritual being; a very wonderful person
angle, *n.* the space between two lines that meet
*Be an **angel** and help me measure this **angle**.*

anyway, *adv.* in any case; at least
any way, in any manner
*Anyway, my teacher told me to do the homework **any way** I knew how.*

bibliography, *n.* a list of books or articles on a particular subject
biography, *n.* an account of a person's life
*On our **bibliography** of heroines, we should include the **biography** of Mother Teresa.*

breath, *n.* air that is taken into the lungs and let out again
breathe, *v.* to take air into the lungs and let it out again
*With each **breath** you take in the country, you **breathe** fresh air.*

cease, *v.* to put an end to; to stop
seize, *v.* to take hold of suddenly and forcibly
*Either **cease** those actions or I'll order the guards to **seize** you.*

coma, *n.* a state of deep unconsciousness caused by disease or injury
comma, *n.* a punctuation mark
*My English teacher practically goes into a **coma** when someone leaves out a **comma**.*

command, *v.* to order; to direct; to be in control of
commend, *v.* to speak highly of; to praise
*If you're brave enough to **command** those wild three-year-olds, I **commend** you.*

confident, *adj.* self-assured; certain
confidant, *n.* a person in whom one can confide
I am confident that I can trust you as my confidant.

conscience, *n.* the awareness of right and wrong
conscious, *adj.* awake and able to feel and think
Listen to your conscience, and you'll be more conscious of right and wrong.

cooperation, *n.* a working together for a common purpose
corporation, *n.* an organization of people who act as one person
We need more cooperation between the chocolate corporation and the peanut butter corporation.

continual, *adj.* frequently repeating (but stopping from time to time)
continuous, *adj.* without interruption; never stopping
The continual barking of the dog and the continuous banging of the radiator kept them up all night.

costume, *n.* clothing worn in a play, circus, etc.
custom, *n.* a habit; a usual practice
Wearing this colorful costume on holidays is a custom in his country.

diseased, *adj.* having or affected by a sickness or illness
deceased, *adj.* dead
Last time we spoke you told me your cat was diseased, now I'm afraid to ask — is he deceased?

decent, *adj.* proper and respectable
descent, *n.* the action of going down
Your behavior should be decent on our descent to Quiet Valley.

desert, *n.* a hot, dry, sandy region with little plant or animal life
dessert, *n.* the last course of a meal, usually a sweet food
In the hot desert, you can't get a frozen dessert or it will melt immediately.

illicit, *adj.* illegal; not permitted by law
elicit, *v.* to bring out; to draw forth
The police tried to elicit answers about illicit drug smuggling.

emigrate, *v.* to go out of one country to live in another
immigrate, *v.* to enter a country to live there
I will emigrate from Italy so I can immigrate into the United States.

eminent, *adj.* outstanding, notable; distinguished above all others
imminent, *adj.* about to happen; impending; threatening
The eminent professor is aware of an imminent disaster if he doesn't hand the papers back before vacation.

farther, *adv.* at a greater physical distance
further, *adj.* additional; to a more advanced point
I'll have to travel farther to make further progress on my research.

finally, *adv.* at last; in conclusion
finely, *adv.* in a very precise way; in small pieces
Finally we found thread spun finely enough to sew dolls' clothes.

formerly, *adv.* in time past; previously
formally, *adv.* in a stiff, proper, polite, or official manner
The woman who was formerly the ambassador came dressed very formally.

hearty, *adj.* full of warmth, affection, friendliness, and kindness
hardy, *adj.* strong; robust; tough; able to endure harsh conditions
I was given a hearty welcome by the hardy couple.

human, *adj.* of or relating to human beings
humane, *adj.* showing sympathy, kindness, mercy, and compassion
A good human being is always humane to other living things.

incredible, *adj.* so strange or unsual that it is unbelievable
incredulous, *adj.* feeling doubt or disbelief
She told such an incredible tale, it's no wonder I was incredulous.

latter, *adj.* being the second of two things referred to
later, *adj.* coming after the expected time
I won't say who was later to school, but, of Adam and Eric, the latter didn't even make lunch time!

lay, *v.* to put something down (always followed by a direct object)
lie, *v.* to place oneself in a resting position (never followed by a direct object)
Do not lay your head on the ground when you lie on the grass.

lose, *v.* to misplace; to fail to win
loose, *adj.* not firmly attached
You will probably lose your loose tooth any minute.

magnate, *n.* a person of great wealth or power in a field or activity

magnet, *n.* a piece of metal that attracts or repels iron or steel

The industrial **magnate** won the award for developing the super **magnet**.

moral, *adj.* good in behavior or character

morale, *n.* the attitude or spirit of a person or a group

It is **moral** to keep the **morale** of your employees high.

persecute, *v.* to treat someone cruelly or harmfully again and again

prosecute, *v.* to bring a person before a court of law

If you try to **persecute** them by withholding their dessert for the third day in a row, I will **prosecute** you for your cruelty.

personal, *adj.* private; relating to a particular person

personnel, *n.* people working in a business

He would rather not have the entire **personnel** department know his **personal** problem.

picture, *n.* a drawing, painting, or photograph

pitcher, *n.* a baseball player who throws the ball to the batter; also a container for holding and pouring liquids

I took a great **picture** of the **pitcher** drinking from a **pitcher** at the end of the game.

precede, *v.* to go in front of someone or something

proceed, *v.* to move forward; to go on with something after stopping

Precede me into the room, so we can **proceed** with the meeting.

preposition, *n.* a word that shows the relationship between words

proposition, *n.* a suggested scheme or plan

He made a **proposition** that we change the **preposition** from "on" to "in".

quite, *adv.* completely; entirely

quiet, *adj.* making no sound; with little noise; peaceful; still

quit, *v.* to stop; to leave one's job.

It has gotten **quite** noisy at work, and if things don't get **quiet**, I'll **quit**.

set, *v.* to put something in a place
sit, *v.* to rest the lower body with the weight off the feet
Set down your packages and sit for a while.

sweet, *adj.* having a pleasant taste like honey or sugar
suite, *n.* connected rooms
In my dream I had a mountain of sweet foods delivered to me in a big hotel suite.

then, *adv.* at that time
than, *conj.* in comparison with
She stuck her tongue out at him, and then he said that he was smarter than she was. What a fight!

thorough, *adj.* all that is needed; complete; perfect
through, *prep.* from one end to the other
Sherlock Holmes conducted a thorough investigation of the crime by searching through every desk in the place.

umpire, *n.* a person who rules on the plays in a sport or game
empire, *n.* a group of countries under one government
On his vacation, the umpire visited the British empire.

DESERT / DESSERT

Contractions: Shrinking Words

A **contraction** is one word that was once two. When you make a contraction, you squeeze together (or contract) two words into one.

Contractions help speed up your speaking and make it sound more natural. You can also use contractions in your writing, especially in a letter to a friend or when you write conversations, dialogue, or direct quotations. However, try not to use contractions too much in reports, research papers, and more formal writing.

SEE ALSO
Apostrophes,
p. 84

How to Make a Contraction

To make a contraction, you leave out one or more letters from the original two words and replace them with an apostrophe ('). Put the apostrophe exactly in the place of the missing letter or letters.

Common Contractions

Contractions		Pronouns + Verbs
I'm	=	I am
I'd	=	I would; I had
I'll	=	I will
I've	=	I have

you'll	=	you will
you'd	=	you would; you had
you've	=	you have
you're	=	you are

he'll	=	he will
he'd	=	he would; he had
he's	=	he is; he has

she'll	=	she will
she'd	=	she would; she had
she's	=	she is; she has

it'll	=	it will
it'd	=	it would; it had
it's	=	it is; it has

we've	=	we have
we'd	=	we would; we had
we'll	=	we will
we're	=	we are

they'll	=	they will
they'd	=	they would; they had
they've	=	they have
they're	=	they are

who's	=	who is; who has
who'd	=	who would; who had

that'll	=	that will
that'd	=	that would; that had
that's	=	that is; that has
let's	=	let us (Verb + Pronoun)

It's and Its

Don't confuse the contraction **it's**

It's (it is) *my favorite song.*

with the possessive pronoun **its.**

The song lost its (the song's) *beat in the middle.*

The contraction has an apostrophe and the pronoun does not.

MORE ➡

Contractions   Verb + *not*

Contractions		Verb + *not*
aren't	=	are not
can't	=	cannot
couldn't	=	could not
didn't	=	did not
doesn't	=	does not
don't	=	do not
hadn't	=	had not
hasn't	=	has not
haven't	=	have not
isn't	=	is not
mustn't	=	must not
shouldn't	=	should not
wouldn't	=	would not
wasn't	=	was not
weren't	=	were not
won't	=	will not

Contractions   *There* + verb

Contractions		*There* + verb
there's	=	there is; there has
there'd	=	there would; there had
there'll	=	there will
there've	=	there have

Contractions   Words + *Is* and *has*

Contractions		Words + *Is* and *has*
what's	=	what is; what has
that's	=	that is; that has
who's	=	who is; who has
here's	=	here is; here has

Building Compound Words

A **compound word** is made up of two or more words. Sometimes one word isn't enough to express an idea, name an object, or say what a speaker or writer is trying to express, so people make up compound nouns and adjectives. Compounds come three ways:

▶ **Closed:** written as one word
▶ **Open:** words written separately
▶ **Hyphenated:** words joined by a hyphen (a short line)

Here are some common compound nouns and adjectives:

Closed Compounds	Open Compounds	Hyphenated Compounds
backyard	best seller	air-conditioned
barefoot	box office	all-purpose
blueberry	cough drop	best-selling
bookstore	day care	break-in
classmate	dining room	check-in
flashlight	hair coloring	drive-in
granddaughter	high school	editor-in-chief
greenhouse	life preserver	follow-up
homework	milk shake	full-length
motorcycle	pencil sharpener	left-handed
paperback	post office	long-distance
textbook	seat belt	play-by-play
touchdown	study hall	tax-free

These words are usually written with hyphens:

▶ All fractions written out in words:

one-half   two-thirds   five-eighths   three-fourths

SEE ALSO
Hyphens,
p. 90

▶ All two-word numbers from twenty-one to ninety-nine written out as words:

thirty-three   fifty-six   forty-nine   ninety-five

▶ Most compounds that begin with **self**:

self-employed self-esteem self-taught self-control

▶ Some two- or three-word family members:

great-aunt   mother-in-law   step-brother

How To Make Compound Nouns Plural

▶ To make most one-word and two-word compound nouns plural, just add **s** to the end:

briefcases   boyfriends   covered wagons   launch pads

▶ With hyphenated compound nouns, make the most important word plural:

great-grandsons   sisters-in-law   passers-by

Idioms:
When Words Mean More Than They Say

An **idiom** is a phrase with a special meaning. Often the meaning has very little (or absolutely nothing) to do with the actual meanings of the words taken one by one. For example, if you tell someone she just "laid an egg," you don't mean that she's a hen. You mean that she just suffered a big failure. "Laid an egg" used this way is an idiom.

If you hear or see an idiom that you don't understand, try looking the key word up in a dictionary. For instance, if you want to know what a "skeleton in the closet" means, look up "skeleton." You'll find that the idiom means having a secret that you don't want anyone to find out.

If the expression isn't in the dictionary, you might find a book in your school or local library that explains idioms.

Here are some common idioms and their explanations:

▶ The teacher's bark is worse than his bite, so don't worry.
(What he says sounds much worse than what he'll do.)

▶ If I'm wrong about this, I'll eat my words.
(If I made a mistake, I'll admit it.)

▶ That new kid really gets under my skin.
(He really annoys me a lot.)

▶ After her big science experiment fizzled, she had egg on her face.
(She was very embarrassed in public.)

▶ We've got to help each other because we're all in the same boat.

(We're in the same bad situation together.)

▶ This new song *you wrote* is going to knock their socks off!

(It will amaze and excite them in a way they didn't expect.)

▶ With this evidence against him, he won't have a leg to stand on.

(He won't have any facts to support his case.)

▶ Uh, oh! Looks like we're out of the frying pan and into the fire!

(We're going from a bad situation into an even worse one.)

▶ Do it yourself, and don't try to pass the buck onto me.

(Don't try to shift the responsibility.)

▶ The bus is leaving, so *you'd* better shake a leg.

(Hurry up. Move fast.)

▶ No matter what they say to convince you to do it, stick to your guns.

(Hold on to your own ideals, even when people try to persuade you to change.)

▶ He swallowed *my* excuse hook, line, and sinker.

(He believed everything I said without question or doubt.)

Clichés
....

Some idioms are also clichés. A **cliché** (pronounced "clee-SHAY") is a popular saying that is used so often by so many people that it gets over-used. Most good writers and speakers avoid using clichés and try to make up new, imaginative expressions of their own.

Initials, Acronyms, and Abbreviations

Initials

Initials are a kind of abbreviation. Sometimes expressions or the names of things are known by their initials (their first letters). These initials take the place of the whole name or word. Here are some of the most common.

A.D.	Anno Domini (Latin for "In the year of our Lord"); any year from 1 on (*The king was born in A.D. 1640.*)
a.m. or A.M.	*ante meridiem* (Latin for "before noon"); the time from midnight to noon
ASAP	As soon as possible
ASPCA	American Society for the Prevention of Cruelty to Animals
B.A.	Bachelor of Arts; a college degree
B.C.	Before Christ; any year before the year 1. British Columbia
B.C.E.	Before the Common Era; any time before the year 1
B.S.	Bachelor of Science; a college degree
C	Celsius; a way to measure temperature (See also **F**)
CD-ROM	Compact Disk-Read Only Memory

CIA	Central Intelligence Agency; branch of the federal government that gathers information about other countries
C.O.D.	Collect (or cash) on Delivery when the package arrives
CTW	Children's Television Workshop
D.A.	District Attorney
D.C.	District of Columbia; as in Washington, D.C.
e.g.	*exempli gratia* (Latin for "for example")
ERA	Equal Rights Amendment
etc.	*et cetera* (Latin for "and so forth," "and others")
F	Fahrenheit; a measurement of temperature (See Also **C**)
FBI	Federal Bureau of Investigation; branch of federal government that investigates crime
GI	Government Issue; nickname for a soldier (Origin: the government issued everything a soldier needed — uniform, weapons, etc.)
HQ	Headquarters
IRS	Internal Revenue Service; the federal government agency that collects income taxes
M.A.	Master of Arts; a college degree
M.D.	Doctor of Medicine; a medical doctor's degree
m.p.h.	miles per hour
MIA	Missing in Action; a lost fighter during war
MTV	Music Television
NAACP	National Association for the Advancement of Colored People
N.B.A.	National Basketball Association

N.H.L.	National Hockey League
N.F.L.	National Football League
p.m. or P.M.	*post meridiem* (Latin for "after noon"); noon to midnight
P.O.	Post Office
PA	Public Address; loudspeaker system
PC	Personal Computer
POW	Prisoner of War; a fighter captured by the enemy in a war
P.S.	Postscript; a note written after the close of a letter
R.N.	Registered Nurse
R.I.P.	Rest in Peace; often written on a gravestone
RR	Railroad
RSVP	*Repondez s'il vous plait*; French for "Please Respond," often put on invitations
RV	Recreational vehicle
SAT	Scholastic Assessment Test; a college entrance exam
TLC	Tender loving care; an expression
UFO	Unidentified flying object
UN or U.N.	United Nations
VIP	Very important person

Acronyms

An **acronym** is a kind of abbreviation. It is a word made out of the first letters of other words. Acronyms never have periods, and they are almost always written out in all capital letters. Here are some of the most common.

AIDS	Acquired Immune Deficiency Syndrome
AWOL	Absent without official leave
CORE	Congress of Racial Equality
HUD	Housing and Urban Development
JEEP	(G.P. vehicle) General Purpose
MADD	Mothers Against Drunk Driving
SADD	Students Against Drunk Driving
MASH	Mobile Army Surgical Hospital
NASA	National Aeronautics and Space Administration
NATO	North Atlantic Treaty Organization
NOW	National Organization for Women
OPEC	Organization of Petroleum Exporting Countries
PIN	Personal Identification Number
RADAR	Radio Detecting and Ranging
SALT	Strategic Arms Limitation Talks
SCUBA	Self-contained Underwater Breathing Apparatus
SNAFU	Situation normal, all fouled up
SONAR	Sound navigation ranging
SWAK	Sealed with a kiss
SWAT	Special Weapons Action Team or Special Weapons and Tactics
UNESCO	United Nations Educational, Scientific, and Cultural Organization
UNICEF	United Nations International Children's Education Fund
VISTA	Volunteers in Service to America
WAC	Women's Army Corps
WHO	World Health Organization
ZIP	Zone Improvement Plan

Abbreviations

To speed up your writing, you may sometimes use a shortened form (**abbreviation**) of a word or phrase. You usually put a period at the end of an abbreviation, but sometimes you don't. If in doubt, check the list below or your dictionary.

State Abbreviations

Use postal abbreviations on addresses in letters and on envelopes. Use the standard abbreviations for all formal writing.

	Postal	Standard		Postal	Standard
Alabama	AL	Ala.	Montana	MT	Mont.
Alaska	AK	Alaska	Nebraska	NE	Neb.
Arizona	AZ	Ariz.	Nevada	NV	Nev.
Arkansas	AR	Ark.	New Hampshire	NH	N.H.
California	CA	Calif.	New Jersey	NJ	N.J.
Colorado	CO	Colo.	New Mexico	NM	N.M.
Connecticut	CT	Conn.	New York	NY	N.Y.
Delaware	DE	Del.	North Carolina	NC	N.C.
Dist. of Columbia	DC	D.C.	North Dakota	ND	N.D.
Florida	FL	Fla.	Ohio	OH	Ohio
Georgia	GA	Ga.	Oklahoma	OK	Okla.
Guam	GU	Guam	Oregon	OR	Ore.
Hawaii	HI	Hawaii	Pennsylvania	PA	Pa.
Idaho	ID	Idaho	Puerto Rico	PR	P.R.
Illinois	IL	Ill.	Rhode Island	RI	R.I.
Indiana	IN	Ind.	South Carolina	SC	S.C.
Iowa	IA	Iowa	South Dakota	SD	S.D.
Kansas	KS	Kan.	Tennessee	TN	Tenn.
Kentucky	KY	Ky.	Texas	TX	Texas
Louisiana	LA	La.	Utah	UT	Utah
Maine	ME	Maine	Vermont	VT	Vt.
Maryland	MD	Md.	Virginia	VA	Va.
Massachusetts	MA	Mass.	Virgin Islands	VI	V.I.
Michigan	MI	Mich.	Washington	WA	Wash.
Minnesota	MN	Minn.	West Virginia	WV	W.Va.
Mississippi	MS	Miss.	Wisconsin	WI	Wis.
Missouri	MO	Mo.	Wyoming	WY	Wyo.

How to Use Abbreviations

Abbreviations are never used as words by themselves. They always go along with other words or names.

They live on a pretty **street.**
Deliver this to 34 Oakdale **St.**

Tomorrow we climb the **mountain.**
Few people have ever climbed **Mt.** Everest.

It can be very cold in **February.**
He was born on **Feb.** 14, 1972.

Common Abbreviations

Here are other common abbreviations. Almost all end with periods.

Adm.	Admiral	**Capt.**	Captain
anon.	anonymous	**cm.**	centimeters
apt.	apartment	**Cpl.**	Corporal
assoc.	associate	**Co.**	Company
asst.	assistant	**Col.**	Colonel
atty.	attorney	**Comdr.**	Commander
Aug.	August	**cont.**	continued
Ave.	avenue	**Corp.**	Corporation
Bldg.	Building	**Dec.**	December
Blvd.	Boulevard	**Dept.**	Department

Dr.	Doctor; Drive	**No.**	number; north
etc.	and others, and so forth (Latin: *et cetera*)	**Nov.**	November
		Oct.	October
	Note: Always put a comma in front of **etc.**	**oz.**	ounces
		p. ; pp.	page; pages
Feb.	February	**Ph.D.**	Doctor of Philosophy
ft.	foot (feet)		
Gen.	General	**Pky. or Pkwy.**	Parkway
Gov.	Governor	**Pres.**	President
in.	inches	**Prof.**	Professor
Inc.	Incorporated	**pt.**	pints
Jan.	January	**Pvt.**	Private
Jr.	junior	**qt.**	quarts
kg.	kilogram	**Rd.**	Road
km.	kilometer	**Rep.**	Representative
lat.	latitude	**Rev.**	Reverend
lb., lbs.	pound, pounds	**Sen.**	Senator
long.	longitude	**Sept.**	September
Ltd.	Limited	**Sgt.**	Sergeant
Maj.	Major	**Sr.**	Senior; Sister
misc.	miscellaneous	**St.**	Street; Saint
ml.	milliliter(s)	**supt.**	superintendent
Mt.	Mountain; Mount	**vol.**	volume
		vs. or v.	versus, opposing
		yd.; yds.	yard; yards

If the last word in a sentence is an abbreviation with a period, you don't have to use another period to end the sentence.

For additional information, write to Freedman Pharmaceuticals, Inc.

Index

Index

Index